You Can't Fall Off The Floor

The rags-to-riches story of a team disrupting the entire insurance industry.

Jamie Prickett

Cataloged in publication information is available from Library and Archives
U.S.
Paperback ISBN: 978-1-956257-33-5
eBook ISBN: 978-1-956257-34-2
Formatting, publishing, cover design by Pierucci Publishing
Interior design by Sophie Hanks
Edited by Dale Chaplin
Cover design by Heather Marine

Dedication

I want to dedicate this book to my haters. I used to wake up angry at you, but today I wake up grateful that you've given me something to fight for and given fuel to my fire. Because of every slimy pyramid scheme out there and every insurance agency that over-promises and under-delivers, my wife Lee-Ann and I have created a better model that unlocks financial freedom for entrepreneurs in record time with record results.

Because of every nasty ex-husband out there, I fight to help the single moms on our team become financially free. Because of every parent who deserves to provide an amazing opportunity for their children and grandchildren. Because of every person who has been duped into a "business opportunity" and was made to feel they weren't good enough to win, I fight for you!

I fight for the agents who come to Experior from other agencies, broken and exhausted from years, or even decades, of false promises and not making ends meet.

I dedicate my life to my agents, but I'm fueled by the haters who said I couldn't do it. Thank you, 'ya filthy animals.

I dedicate this book to my wife, Lee-Ann. You are a true leader and the light of our family. Our agents adore you. You truly are the most amazing, sweetest, and smartest woman in the world. The night you told me that God had a bigger plan for us after we lost Empirical Group, you once again showed that you're a spiritual leader, too. Thank you for introducing me to our Father in Heaven and helping me defeat all of the Goliaths we've come across together. I love you, babe!

Contents

Part Three: Keys To Creating a Great Company

Before You Read...

If you're reading this book, you probably want to know how my wife Lee-Ann and I are bringing a stuffy, bloated, cutthroat, and largely dishonest financial services industry to its knees. You want the inspirational, rags-to-riches story about how a couple of struggling entrepreneurs built a company with over 1,700 business owners working with us; a number that is steadily growing every day. You may want to hear the stories of how everyone from immigrants, the downtrodden, and even folks in their sixties and seventies have built one, two, and five-million-dollar businesses, some of whom are now earning up to half a million dollars annually (soon to be in the millions) of passive income through our revolutionary model that compensates the agents more than other companies dare to part with. And finally, you may be reading this book because you're simply curious to learn more about how to apply the principles we've used to skyrocket Experior Financial Group to one of the fastest-growing companies in Canada and the U.S.

Foreword

"Jamie, what's that noise?" My wife Lee-Ann mutters through her "make-up face." It's the duckface one where you pout your lips while sucking in your cheekbones to apply blusher and lip gloss.

"I don't know, babe. You just worry about you and I'll get us there on time, we're ten minutes away. Lee-Ann, you look beautiful without the make-up, you know." I wink, but she doesn't see. Lee-Ann doesn't wear a lot of make-up. She doesn't need to. She's got ocean-blue eyes and a smile that lights up a room... She's not worried about make-up as much as she is about the complexion of her heart. That's one of a million things I love about her.

The alarming noise our car made instantly goes from a scratch to a deafening screech. Lee-Ann has a shocked look on her face, which could be from the mascara, or it could be due to the noise.

"Jamie, something isn't right." This is now quite clear as it sounds like we are driving a rocket ship.

I impulsively reach over and smack the mascara out of Lee-Ann's fingers before screeching to a quick stop on the side of the road, worried our brakes might give out alongside everything else that's falling apart in the beat-up old car that we somehow managed to keep on the road, despite it well exceeding 400,000 km (250,000 miles for my American friends).

I throw my tie over my shoulder and catch a whiff of the cologne that I hesitated about spritzing on before we left. While Lee-Ann gave instructions to the babysitter for our three children at the time (our fourth came shortly after), I had gotten ready by preparing my speech for the night's event: a celebration of the many successful insurance agents at the large firm where Lee-Ann and I worked. Somehow, even with this beat-up car and the craziness of our blended household, we were scheduled to be on stage at the event; to be celebrated. "For what?" I wondered.

The event felt like a sham, even though I knew Lee-Ann and I weren't disingenuous by any degree with that company. We just weren't making ends meet. Tonight, while driving to a city just outside of our hometown, spending our grocery money on gas, the accolades for our accomplishments verged on ridiculous. I was literally going to be on stage sharing our "success," but in reality, although I was selling the dream, we were living a nightmare.

On this rainy fall evening, it didn't feel like living the dream. I wanted my wife to get dolled up for a steak dinner, not an industry event and charade. I wanted to pull up in a Mercedes with leather seats, not this hunk of junk.

After ten years with the company we were with, which we'll refer to in this book as the "Practice Company", I thought I'd be a millionaire by now, not trudging through puddles in my already thread-bare shoes to retrieve my muffler and exhaust pipe, which both decided to abandon me before my on-stage self-betrayal. It didn't stop me that night, and it doesn't stop me now.

I tip-toed through some grey puddles towards the rear of my car and proceeded to yank on the exhaust, which had come apart just enough to send a shower of sparks if I continued down the road. The car behind us had stopped and a man helped me yank on the exhaust until it finally came off, and we threw it to the side of the road.

"Hey, man, thanks for your help. I'm so sorry. Are you okay?"

"I was about to ask you the same thing," the man says, staring at my mud-soaked shoes and poorly fitted suit that I purchased from Value Village (a secondhand thrift store in Canada). I hope he didn't smell that cologne. I knew it was a poor choice.

When I get back in the car, Lee-Ann, who has held her composure through many difficult moments in the Prickett household, simply states, "Well I hope he isn't going to be at the conference."

"I've got more bad news, babe. We need gas," I say while motioning my head towards the glaring orange fuel tank light on our dashboard.

"Okay, I'll call the bank," Lee-Ann says stoically. I can tell she's working hard to keep a straight face, or at least not to cry and muddy up her mascara the way I just muddied up my suit retrieving the muffler and exhaust pipe.

"Hello, this is Lee-Ann Prickett," Lee-Ann says in a wavering voice. The voice on the other end knows exactly what this call is about.

"Oh, hi Lee-Ann! Let me check for you..." There was a pause. "You have seven dollars, four cents in the checking, and zero in the savings."

"Thanks, Mary." Lee-Ann mutters, defeated, "Seven dollars. No coffee at the convention, Jamie."

I pull into the gas station and fill up five dollars in the tank; just enough to get us into the city and back out to our home in the Guelph suburbs.

"We can share a coffee," I say optimistically when I get back into the car.

For ten years this was my routine almost every day. I called the bank from the gas pump to find out what was in my checking account. Being an insurance salesman I drove a lot, making house calls. For ten years I filled up my tank with five or ten dollars a time, depending on what I had in the account. I'll never forget how settled my stomach felt on days I filled it up with twenty dollars. I wouldn't have to drive home trying to avoid any abrupt starts, aiming to preserve gas. I could relax a moment, and maybe even avoid the gas pump for a couple of days. Just maybe...

For ten years I drove vehicles that were so run down that one time a man came to our door and asked me about a minivan we had in the driveway. Seemed he wanted to purchase it.

"It's not for sale, but I'm open to offers," I explained.

"Oh, well, you see we're doing a demolition derby in town this weekend and we're looking for some vehicles."

That minivan, however, didn't last much longer. Once the door even fell off when my son Hayden opened it. Thankfully, I was putting another five dollars of gas in when he yanked the sliding door open. Somehow, I caught the door before he could finish saying "whoa!" For a few more months, our four kids used the sliding door on the other side of the van.

It wasn't always a 10,000 square foot house with an indoor swimming pool for the Prickett family. We weren't always blessed with flash cars either; we didn't always have the McLaren, the multiple S-Class Mercedes, or a Bentley that I didn't love quite as much as my Mercedes S-Class, so I sold it at some point during the writing of this book. It wasn't always a net worth of millions of dollars more than my entire family had made in about a thousand years. And it wasn't always 1,700 (and counting) licensed insurance agents in my company.

Nay, there was a time when Lee-Ann and I were fighting over ketchup. Well, I remember that it was ketchup. She recalls that it was cereal. She came home from shopping for the week one night and, from the corner of my eye, seemed to scamper past the living room. And she's not generally a sneaky person...

Our budget at the time was $50 for five people per *week,* which we only increased to $60 when our youngest was born a short time thereafter.

"Lee-Ann, what's going on?" I asked as I entered the kitchen. Lee-Ann jumped a mile high, and that's when I became concerned. I looked at her grocery bags for something that she could be hiding.

"Heinz Ketchup?! Who really needs to slather their food with sugar sauce of such prestige? Lee-Ann, was that really necessary? Cheap, no-name brands taste just as good at a fraction of the cost. Why didn't you get the ketchup at the Dollar Store?"

A fight ensued. About ketchup. Damn, I can't believe she didn't walk out the door right then and there.

Lee-Ann and I once took a course by Dave Ramsey in those

days at the Practice Company when we were barely making ends meet. One of Dave's strategies was to sell stuff in your house that you don't need. I remember his joking line: "Sell so much stuff that the kids think they're next!"

We took his advice so seriously that we sold the kids' bedframes and even sold our couch to keep up with running our businesses, to pay for our office and licensing fees with the Practice Company, as well as to put gas in those horrid beat-up cars. When people came to the house during that period, we explained that it was empty because we were remodeling. If they'd ask about my car, both quizzically and disapprovingly, I'd explain that Lee-Ann told me I could get any car I wanted if I got my car to reach 400,000 km. Well, I made it to that number, but instead of a new car, the junkyard rewarded me with $200 that I put back into the infamous minivan with the broken door.

Today, eleven years after the infamous ketchup fight and eight years since we started our own agency, Experior Financial Group, my wife doesn't have a budget for groceries, cars, or vacations; she certainly doesn't have a personal shopping budget.

Did we win the lottery? Absolutely.

We won the lottery. And in this book, I'm going to give you the winning numbers, or letters, as it may be.

H-U-S-H.

The hush is that beautiful moment in a sports arena when the basketball player shoots for a three-pointer just before the buzzer. Even the opposing team can't help but stare wide-eyed, silent, jaws dropped. *Will he do it?*

Yes, he will. So did I. And so can you.

HUSH stands for:

- Haters are fuel
- Underdog advantage
- Stay in the fight
- Hope

This is my winning recipe for, well, winning. In this book, I'll give you concrete, actionable steps to help you win too. You'll learn about greatness through the eyes of my teammates, without whom I wouldn't have been able to pull this great heist of the entire insurance MGA/IMO world off. In Part One, you'll learn a bit about how we built Experior, or, rather, built up ourselves enough to create it. In Part Two, you'll see through the eyes of the teammates who helped build Experior and what leadership qualities we consider to be inextricably linked to our success. In Part Three, we'll give you guidelines for creating a leading company in your industry, just like we've done with Experior Financial Group.

Neither Lee-Ann nor I were born with silver spoons, although we do have a lot of love and respect for where we came from. We have even more love for where we are now; for what we've created, and the impact we have had on so many people. It's been suggested by great thinkers and philosophers, such as Jordan Peterson, that each generation is more conscious than their parents, resulting in things such as fewer abused children. The characters you'll meet in this book are evidence of this evolving consciousness in humanity and, especially, in business. You'll meet over twenty of our Executive Directors from within Experior Financial Group. They aren't just business leaders and partners, they're some of our dearest friends.

In fact, I'd rather kick it with my wife, my four kids, or our agents any day, than flaunt my Rolex in some stuffy-looking golfer's gear.

It's a badge of honor to spend an evening revving up sales teams and hearing everybody say afterward, one after another, "That was awesome, man! You've changed my life!" Success hasn't lured me away from what and who counts.

This book is going to reveal a winning formula from a real guy who neither went to the fancy prep schools nor got his start as an independently wealthy or otherwise well-bred trust funder. The team you'll meet in this book isn't altogether polished either, but they are absolutely powerful. If we can do it, so can you.

Experior Financial Group wasn't funded with handfuls of investors or partners with mountainous books of business to pillage. We certainly didn't fund it with a year or two of rainy-day funds so that we could get on our feet.

It was me, Lee-Ann, a lot of guts, a lot of grace, and a lot of hope.

There wasn't time or money to "get on our feet" when we started Experior. But the reason we are where we are now is that we were always on our feet, especially when we didn't even have a couch to sit on. We've never backed down. We've never quit.

We don't play the victim or ask "why." Rather, we ask "why not?"

So why shouldn't you?

Introduction

"The only thing more difficult than the emotional toil of pursuing true excellence is the emotional toil of not pursuing true excellence."
Steven Kotler

"You don't have to have religion in order to succeed, but you must have faith."
Jamie Prickett

Lee-Ann and I have experienced an exponential rise from the days of calling up the bank to put five bucks of fuel in our beater of a car to where we are now. In just eight years, my wife and President of Experior and I have absolutely built the greatest insurance agency on the planet, with the greatest agents. You may disagree with me, but this is my book, and I believe it with my whole heart.

The principles and stories in this book will reference that meteoric rise from what I call living for "gas and groceries" to "gold and glory." It's the rags-to-riches story of a husband and wife who built an enterprise from the ground up with a family of four to raise. It's the story of how Lee-Ann and I created a company from non-existence to one of the top ten insurance agencies in Canada and, at the time of writing this book, we're in 38 states in the U.S., but it should be all 50 by the time you've finished reading.

From the start, Lee-Ann and I have broken many molds. You see, the average age of insurance agents in Experior is actually about forty years old, and it is about 60-one years old across the industry. In the U.S., there are more licensed agents over the age of eighty than under the age of thirty. Why is this industry so old? Well, mostly because the industry is not training "greenies" anymore. Rather they are chasing the fat-cats that have been selling insurance since the earth cooled. You need a cushion since it's traditionally a waste of time to over-promise a kid out of college that they're going to hit six figures of income in their first year. Does it happen? Absolutely, but those cases are unicorns. The beauty of our company is that we embrace part-time agents that are serious about transitioning to full-time.

It just so happens that Experior has a lot of unicorns. We're underdogs though. There isn't a person in this book that you're going to read about who hasn't broken a mold - not just in our company - but in our industry as a whole. Insurance is simply an old-dog industry. I have spoken at a few industry conferences to a sea of blinding white hair, mostly men who were also white-skinned. It felt like I was looking at clouds from above. Everything about it felt... well... white-washed. As any of you reading this should know, we've done things differently, and in this day and age, if you truly want to make an impact; doing things differently is imperative.

Experior typically has about two or three white guys in our top twenty-five producers each month. We love diversity; we're living proof that when given a chance, all men and women from every nation and creed can be successful. We have men and women who are African American, Asian, Caucasian, Indigenous, Italian, Filipino, Latino... I could go on for a while, but you get the point. We have an average of at least 40% women on our team. I like to say that Experior is like the United Nations.

Who This Book is NOT For...

So, since my formula for success involves an inevitable interface with your haters (lest you become a coddled sally), I'll start by telling you who this book is NOT for. This book is not for people who want tricks to "hack the system." The truth is, Lee-Ann and I didn't get to where we are by hacking any system with mind-numbingly brilliant algorithms and meticulously split-tested Google ads. We got here by building strong relationships with our agents, with our mentors, with each other, and most importantly, with our Creator. I'm not going to preach at you in this book, but I give the Glory to my Creator the Almighty God, and I choose to capitalize these words because I can. Period. You don't have to agree. You can call Him a Her, or Universe, or Gaia, or the Head Honcho in the Clouds, I don't care. This isn't a twelve-step program, and you don't have to have religion in order to succeed, *but you must have faith.*

This book isn't for employees who want to remain employees. It's not for people who love to roll in at 8:59 a.m. and dash out the door at 4:59 p.m. It isn't for those who love being told what to do. It's certainly not for people who choose a consistent paycheck over the insane rush you get when you understand that you can create your own income and that that income is limitless. If you like to choose what you do, where you do it, and with whom you work, this book is for you. 80% of business owners fail in their first five years. I don't think that's because they're unintelligent, or even because they're lazy. I think it's because they don't think like business owners. They don't take personal responsibility for creating their income, managing their time, and writing their own paychecks. They're not *owners*. You'll hear me use this word a lot because it's one of the fundamental reasons Experior has exploded in growth and profitability. Our company is founded on the agents within it operating like owners. They have my support, but the freedom and flexibility to write their own tickets, so to speak, for better or worse.

On that note, this book isn't for wimps. You picked this up because you know you're destined for something great. But on the off-chance that you picked it up at a used book sale and you're trying to decide if you want to crank through it, I want to let you know that it isn't for those of you who struggle to stand in your power. In my business, it's not enough to write an insurance policy for the best price or invest people's money into an annuity with the sexiest brochure. I have to learn about my client and recommend what's right for them, and sometimes, that's not the sexiest option. In fact, sometimes it's much more expensive than what they Googled before our meeting. If you truly love your clients - which I really do - you'll tell them the hard truths that sometimes need to be told and put them into what's right for them and their families, not what pays you the best commission or what Google tells them to do based off of some fictitious avatar.

This book isn't for hermits. That's right, if you want to succeed, you have to get out there and get social. The best thing you can do for your own sanity, as well as that of your family (especially in those first few grueling months when you think you'll never sell a policy, enroll new clients, or offload one of your prize widgets), is to surround yourself with people who've succeeded in your industry. Find a mentor and flatter them by asking if you can pick their brain over breakfast, and you'd love to not just treat them to breakfast but invest in their consulting fee. 99% of the time, these folks are going to be so impressed with your eagerness to learn and glean from them, they wouldn't dream of charging you a fee. But if they do, you'll be even luckier because you'll value their time even more. Don't ask somebody to dinner if you want them to be sharp. High-performing people have sharper minds in the morning than at a dinner that's generally dulled by a drink or two, or by the heaviness of their day. Show this person that you're disciplined enough to meet early before their office hours; show them you respect their busy schedules and don't suggest cutting into their family time. You know the adage that suggests we're the sum of the five people we spend the most time with? Write down a list of those five names right now and I guarantee you'll have some insights into where you are now and why you're there.

This book isn't for know-it-alls. You're not going to do well in insurance, finance, or real estate just because you're a finance major who wakes up with the markets to trade options. In fact, of all the agents who rely on strong interpersonal and social skills on average far outperform those that I've taken from high-brow universities. I'm still learning from my team daily, which not only helps me improve my own skills but also gives me the opportunity to empower my team because they are my teachers and leaders as much as I am theirs.

This book isn't for people who are just "in it for the money." Why? Look, the joy isn't in reaching a financial goal.
"Hey Jamie, you're driving Bentleys and McLarens, who are you to talk?" But you see, I'm equally as motivated now as when I had a back tax bill of $5,000 and didn't know how I was going to pay it. It's crazy to think that that was just seven years ago (shout-out to my mother-in-law, who came through for us with money that she didn't have to spare after our first year of building Experior). But the joy isn't in reaching your goal, it's in consistently setting new goals and striving for ever greater heights.

I've learned that what really gets me high in life, the reason I've avoided depression almost all of my life, and the reason that my business feeds over 1,700 families, is that I've learned this secret about happiness: the joy is in the pursuit. Once the monkey has the banana, the dopamine reward center shuts off until he's in pursuit of another banana. The joy isn't in the reward. It's in the pursuit. If you don't love working for something, this book isn't going to resonate with you, straight up.

This book isn't for people living in scarcity, or people who see the Universe as limited. It isn't for the whiners and complainers who always have an excuse for why they're still hustling for gas and groceries. It's not for people who cannot visualize success because they let their own negative thinking get in the way. We're not exactly having séances and pulling tarot cards before appointments, but my team does think wealthy thoughts, and that's why so many of them, whom you'll meet in the upcoming pages, have gone from penniless to prosperous in record time. I'd love the same for you too.

Look, your subconscious mind picks up on literally everything you say. When people ask me how I feel, I tell them the truth: "I feel like a million bucks" or "any better and I'd be twins." I always have, and I always will. If you want success, you must walk, talk, act, and feel like success. Everything you visualize manifests. The negative woe-is-me victim language has to go, or you'll go insane. If you find yourself playing the world's smallest violin regularly, this is your wake-up call. Your negative self-talk is sabotaging you. I don't think you have to meditate for three hours a day to cultivate positive self-talk, but it is a muscle that you must exercise. If you think you have it in you, buckle up. Let's talk about who this book is for...

Who This Book Is For...

This book is for you if you're ready and willing to earn massive amounts of money to do what you love with whom you love to do it. I know, who could say no to that? But remember, you're going to need to learn to hustle your HUSH with resilience, self-regulation, and, above all, hope.

This book is for owners. Being an owner in your business is multi-faceted. You see, if you own a home and you die, your family gets the home. In the same way, our Experior agents own the agencies they build.

This book is for dreamers. It's one thing to "not wanna work for someone else." It's a whole different nut to crack to have dreams. You won't fail for dreaming big. You'll fail for dreaming small.

This book is for team players. Remember: iron sharpens irons. If you're hanging around a bunch of wet mops, you're staring a bleak future straight in the face. We like to say at Experior: find a foxhole buddy. Success doesn't come without hardships. Your team isn't just your office or your "upline" manager; your team and other people throughout the company are your family as well.

This book is for learners. I'm a learner, in fact, I had to ask my wife Lee-Ann what the words "vignette" and "quintessential" meant just last night. My team is full of learners too. Experior's Executive Director Darren Golka remembers a meeting we had with a handful of veritable celebrities in the insurance industry; men I'd dreamt of joining our growing Experior business back in 2018. Golka remembers how transparent I was in those meetings that we held in the Experior conference room in Guelph, Ontario. As I wooed the room, illustrating how progressive our company was in how we'd taken the very best of every great financial services firm in existence, and married their best attributes into what we call the Tribrid model, Golka spoke up, "Well, what about the comp plan? Do you know what "XYZ" Company does to attract and retain talent?"

I hadn't. I looked over at Lee-Ann, who was staring at Golka square in the eyes. "We're not familiar, please enlighten us." So Golka laid it out for me, having been C-Suite at that company in a previous life. Two weeks later, I called Golka up while Lee-Ann and I were on our first vacation in three years.

"Jamie, why are you calling me? Go enjoy your holiday!"

"No, wait a second. I want you to know that the comp plan changes you suggested have been implemented. Lee-Ann and the kids are out right now. Can you talk?"

"Suggested? I was just sharing. I didn't think you'd take it that seriously!" Needless to say, Golka came on board with Experior and now runs one of the largest organizations in our company with over 650 licensed agents.

"Jamie, you showed me that you're teachable, that you listen, and that you're a leader. I couldn't say no to that. We're going to be a billion-dollar company someday, and it's because of this moment." If you're teachable, there's no ceiling on what you can accomplish. When you hit a wall, you'll figure out how to build a ladder or blast through it in your rocket ship.

A mentor of mine says, "the only way out is through, but the best way through is together." I once read an article from Conscious Lifestyle Magazine, by author Nick Seneca Jenkel, that detailed studies of over 200,000 individuals worldwide who reported deep happiness and satisfaction with life. In every socioeconomic class and every nation, that happiness was brought about by being a part of a tribe, or, as Jenkel says, "connecting with and contributing to others." My team isn't here to write policies, they're here to solve problems and pave the road to financial freedom for families.

If you're in a cut-throat industry, you're going to be right at home here. Being young and penniless was a sure-fire way for me to fail in my own industry. There was nothing worse than asking why "that guy" was able to build a million-dollar business in my former agency. "He got there so quickly and has been coasting through life for the last twenty years! How did he become so successful?" Sadly, in the traditional insurance industry, it can take a few years to start making good money. Even more disheartening is how many successful agents I saw in my last business who achieved success simply by being in the right place at the right time. I felt like I was just a little too late to the party.

What about me? What about everyone else joining in "today's time?" Don't they deserve the same opportunity? Do you think everybody sits around sharing the truth about why and how they had to work far less than you? Or how you will hustle like a slave to achieve a fraction of what they achieved just by showing up at the right time? Do they tell you this in the beginning?

No. It's every man and woman out for themselves. The number of times people that we had at our wedding turned their backs on me when I left the Practice Company to start my own agency with Lee-Ann is staggering, and I'll tell you more about that later in this book.

If you're looking for tips on how to build your insurance business, or any business for that matter, you're in the right place. This is not a book that will provide you with top-secret tools, nor is it the same bad rehash of other business books. You'll learn the precise methods with which I've achieved my success, and it's like nothing you've ever heard. And coincidentally, if you're in any sales or entrepreneurship role whatsoever, you'll never be the same after reading this book.

If you're feeling distraught, dejected, or otherwise anxious about your current professional trajectory, pull up a chair, and if you're a startup entrepreneur looking for inspiration on how to attract, manage, and retain top talent, as we do, you're about to step inside our previously closely-guarded secrets and learn exactly how my team grew Experior to an eight-figure business (that's a lot of zeroes) in just eight years.

Hold on tight, kings and queens. It's about to get real.

Part One

The Road to Greatness (isn't always paved...)

Chapter One

The Tortoise and The Hare

"Once you've wrestled, everything else in life is easy."
Dan Gable

"Experior is one of the best self-development programs out there, and it happens to come with an awesome compensation package attached to it."
Jamie Prickett

Growing up, I only wanted to be a wrestler. My dad had been a wrestler and had drilled into me when my mind was young and impressionable that it was the greatest sport in the world. The problem was that I was short, chubby, and I couldn't run or jump. This made training for my Olympic dreams tough. In the seventh grade, I went hard. I began spending every spare moment I could lifting weights or even offering to take on tough jobs around the house just to train; happily helping Mom with groceries or enthusiastically offering to lift heavy things with every chance I got.

My parents weren't rich either. Dad was a mechanic and Mom was a baker; she later helped my Dad in the mechanic shop. Growing up, I knew that if she came home with boxes instead of plastic bags, it meant she had been to the food bank that week.

I struggled in school, eventually graduating by the skin of my teeth with a D+ average over five years. In fact, the only reason I finished high school was because I wanted to stay on the wrestling team. I'd wrack my brain during math tests, sweating with anxiety when I saw dizzying pages of numbers and equations on standardized tests, which is actually now quite funny to me as my wife and I have built a massive organization because of our understanding of financial instruments (numbers), an outstanding comp plan (more numbers), as well as our winning formulas to grow a company in our industry faster than any of the other 400+ companies in Canada.

In school, I'd turn the zeroes on those tests into little Cheerios and visualize being in the Olympics for wrestling, getting my Cheerios sponsorship. I'd be on a cereal box and one day I'd live off sponsorship money.

The hard work and naive dreaming paid off, despite my dad's tough, take-no-prisoners approach. I took second-place in Canada in high school and fifth in the senior competition two years after high school. I'll never forget returning home after my gold medal match where I lost in the finals and got silver. I remember announcing, "Dad, I just got the silver medal!" His face was surprisingly somber, and he paused a moment, before replying, "I guess the other guy wanted it more than you."

I thought my dad was a real piece of work that night, but I meditated on those words for years to come. I knew I'd trained hard and that 99% of the wrestlers in the country would have loved to get that silver medal; they would have settled for it happily. But for me, and especially for my dad, silver wasn't acceptable. It wasn't a win.

"We have 25 wrestlers on board and a lot of grade nines and that is a really good sign," said Diamond. "We have a lot of good wrestlers and that will take us a long way this year."

Leading the team this year will be Jamie Prickett and Jamie Cox. A lot of pressure will be placed on both these wrestlers to reach OFSAA this year. Prickett is in his last year at the high school and he wants to reach the highest level he can.

"Both of these guys are wrestling great so far," said Diamond. "Prickett has yet to have a point scored on him in two tournaments."

Prickett takes silver at wrestling Nationals; sets sights on berth into Canada Summer Games

Jamie Prickett displays his silver medal

Jamie Prickett finds himself in an awkward position during his match-up with the reigning OFSAA champion at the National Wrestling Championships in Guelph.

My young wrestling career

You'll remember the story of *The Tortoise and the Hare*. In later years, I began to see everything in life as a race for the gold, with this story being the quintessential (see, I'm using big words now Lee-Ann) formula. In the story, the tortoise starts slow, but he's consistent. He doesn't have the ego of the hare, who bursts out of the gate and gets so cocky that he stops to chat with onlookers during the race. He's fast, yeah. He has some natural gifts and even a God-given physique that would make him perfectly suited to win the race against even the most impressive tortoise. But he doesn't have the drive, consistency, and habits of a winner. In fact, his mindset is that of a total loser.

In wrestling, and in business, I've been the tortoise, and it's served me well. It's not solely because nobody will outwork me, but that I also thrive off of the haters and the trash talkers, whom I have always envisioned as being like the hare in that story. I put one foot in front of the other, day after day, going the extra mile and never stopping to congratulate myself before picking myself up for the next race. I'm not the smartest, prettiest, or naturally-advantaged competitor, but with a dedication to my craft and my stubborn unwillingness to give up, I am able to keep moving forward.

Winning is crazy. Let's face it, I had to be borderline crazy to think that I could get to the Olympics based on drive alone. Natural talent wasn't handed to me like it was for the hare. I often say that only 10% of success comes from a skillset, the rest is mindset, and that's how I became fairly successful in wrestling. It's also how I mop the floor in business, and it's how I've led over 1,700 agents in Experior to unlock their dreams as business owners in our organization.

Admittedly, I'm short on skillset, but I am blessed with the right mindset in spades. After high school, I worked for three years in a factory job. Then, I left to work in financial services for what I thought would be a temporary move for six months while I got back on my feet, planning to continue my dream of wrestling after. Turns out, I am still in the industry 20 years later.

I only made $13,000 my first year in the financial industry. I started like the tortoise, but I knew that, unlike in wrestling, business has a level playing field. You can be short, fat, skinny, black, brown, or white. You can have a questionable past, come from the wrong side of the tracks, yet you have the same opportunity to win as if you'd been fed with a silver spoon, coddled in country clubs, and attended all the right private schools.

And guess what? My Experior agents aren't the latter of those two. We've got Executive Directors, like Denesh Logeswaran, whose family came here as refugees and got caught in the crosshairs of neighborhood gang violence. He was even shot twice in the back for chatting with the wrong neighbor at the wrong time. We've got men like Tyrone Hinds, another six-figure earner who just bought a pool for his new home and his wife and three kids, who once heard so many gunshots outside his front door on the wrong side of town that he slept in his daughter's bed; both he and his little girl were too scared to sleep that night. We've got Neela

Mannan, who still chokes up remembering how, in her previous financial services company, she went as far as to sell her jewelry to get by, including pieces she'd brought with her from her home in Dubai, earmarked for her daughters' weddings. In business, it doesn't matter where you come from or how old you are; you can get to where you're going when you believe in yourself.

You may be wondering where my Olympic dreams went. Now, at 42 years old, I'm not going to compete in the Olympics; and a sponsorship from Cheerios wouldn't pay for my vehicles. But I have made it to the Olympic standard in leadership.

When I started with my first insurance company as an agent, I thought I was going to make so many millions so fast that I was going to retire and wrestle. I hung on in that first year, even though I only made $13,000. In the second year, I lost my house because I fell three months behind on mortgage payments. I drove to people's homes for appointments with the Practice Company. I was in such straits that my car wasn't even insured at one point for about six months. To add insult to injury, I went through a divorce during my second year of having the business, right after my second child was born. Having Haylee and Hayden helped cushion the pain; I now had a son and a daughter who needed me, and extra motivation to pull me through a difficult time. An extra reason to persevere.

Believe it or not, I returned to competitive wrestling several years later. Even then, I never lost sight of my dream. I had started drinking and smoking in my mid-to-late-twenties; I was altogether pretty washed up, but I still won fifth place in Canada that year, just to get my head straight whilst several other relationships were going south, before I finally met and married my bride, Lee-Ann, in 2010.

Jamie and Chris Prickett

In 2012, my little brother Chris retired from the sport of wrestling, where he had some major success. He became a two-time national champion, bronze medalist at the Pan-American Games, and an Olympic alternate. Shortly after he retired from the sport, Lee-Ann and I started to experience success with Experior. By 2016, I'd attracted veritable heroes in the industry to build our company with us, including Frank De Lio, Mauro Arturi, and Laval Dubeau. The verdict was still out as to whether or not I was crazy, but they were all-in.

Having taken a decidedly different approach to Chris's success, I spoke to Chris shortly after he won the final match at the Canadian National Championships where, despite being injured, not a single point was scored on him the entire tournament. UNREAL!

"Chris, why are we both able to be successful despite not growing up in a family of sports legends or millionaires?"

Chris didn't skip a beat, "Because nobody wants to put in the daily discipline that's required. They want it to happen fast. When they see the sacrifice that success requires, they make room for guys like us who are willing to put in the daily discipline and consistency. It's the tortoise and the hare, bro..."

Not everybody on my team wins awards every year, but I also don't teach them to need constant pats on the back or participation trophies. Hell, that stuff will ruin you. I teach them leadership the same way I teach our clients about compounding interest (yeah, I still have a few clients whose assets I manage, although they're few and far between these days). A little consistency over time compounds; that's how you develop your dream life.

Text from my mom after my brother Chris' girlfriend Jasmine Jasudavicius won her UFC debut January 22nd, 2022

January 2014. It was Lee-Ann and me, along with six others, sitting around a fold-up table. It was in one room on the second floor of a flower shop, where we had just started Experior. The space was very "rustic" with no parking whatsoever. Not surprisingly, the team looked confused and skeptical. I took a deep breath and spoke. Nah, who am I kidding, I preached. I hooted, hollered, and cheered as though I was on stage at a stadium in front of thousands of agents who'd just made millions of dollars that year. That's what the vision of Experior always was, and that's what is materializing for Lee-Ann and me now.

The Flower Shop we had to go through to get to our second floor office of 300 sq. feet when we launched Experior

The flower shop must have thought that we had a football game blaring as we heard a gentle knock on the wall, like parents reminding a kid to turn down the television. I didn't turn it down. I got louder. At that moment, I heard myself saying that we'd all been through hell, but we had gotten here, and this was our destiny. We'd trudged our respective ways through other companies, with their sleazy practices and broken promises, but Experior was going to be different. Nobody on the planet had what we had, and nobody would have a chance at replicating it. I channeled the same aggression, ambition, and energy that I had in wrestling, and throughout those ten years floundering in the financial industry, plus two more in a company that myself and Lee-Ann started before Experior with partners, for us only to be robbed from and sued. Except now, this time, I was the head coach.

Chapter One Lessons:

#1: Successful people aren't lucky; they succeed because they are willing to put in the daily discipline and consistency that's required. They are the tortoise versus the hare.

#2: Consistency over time compounds.

Chapter Two

Lee-Ann

"Lee-Ann is the softest, sweetest, humblest person I've ever met. She's the ultimate role model for women and men. As the President of our company, she has never made me feel unwanted, invaluable, or like a number to her."
David Longmore, Experior Executive Director

"Don't be fooled: Lee-Ann Prickett is a workhorse.
I worked 24-hour days when I first came to Experior. Lee-Ann worked 25.
Behind-the-scenes, she's the hard-line Jamie needed, but you'll never hear that from her."
Darren Golka, Experior Executive Director

Jamie and Lee-Ann Prickett on stage

You've heard it said that behind every great man is an even greater woman, right? Not in my case; that woman is the President of Experior. She owns as much of Experior as I do. That's right, this book is as much about a team of heroes as it is about the Experior heroines: most notably Lee-Ann Prickett.

Few people know about Lee-Ann's past, but she's infamous throughout our company as the quintessential badass behind-the-scenes. She's just as comfortable sitting with our attorneys and flying around the continent to swoon gigantic men and women in the financial space as she is discussing the five love languages with her team. Few people know how Lee-Ann cut her chops as this proverbial Jane-of-all-trades and fewer know how she keeps such a gentle countenance with me as her husband and business partner. Anybody on the team will tell you, especially Frank De Lio and Darren Golka, that I've been known to explode a bit as I've grown and homed in my own emotional intelligence. That shit didn't come from YouTube videos; it came from gleaning the natural confidence and wise, stoic nature of my wife.

Lee-Ann's parents separated when she was thirteen and her dad moved out. Her mom couldn't pay their bills, so Lee-Ann dropped out of school around the age of sixteen to work in a jewelry store and help her mom pay them. Due to her dad's mental health issues and permanent disability status, he didn't contribute to Lee-Ann and her mom's home. Even as a University of Guelph administrator, times were tough for Mom and the three kids (Lee-Ann being the middle child). Her mom paid us back when we needed it most. When we started Experior, we were renting our home with four children. One year after starting Experior, we owed $5,000 in taxes. Lee-Ann's mom made a massive sacrifice and paid that bill for us, and we'll never forget her being there when we needed her most.

I love the fact that Lee-Ann and I come from the humblest of beginnings and even humbler educations, yet we've built one of the top insurance agencies in all of Canada. When we tell our agents that they can do it, they are wise to study mine and Lee-Ann's lives before they pick up a book about some Silicon Valley trust-funder who had parents introducing them to VCs at their college graduations. We're the real deal, but mostly Lee-Ann is.

Lee-Ann and I met in 2007 at the Practice Company where we both worked, a company that later sued us as I briefly mentioned earlier (more on that later). By 2009, I just had to go on a date with Lee-Ann. There was an allure to her kindness and purity, and part of me simply couldn't wait to see her let go a little.

With business, as with romance, Lee-Ann won. I didn't tarnish the good girl; rather, she had me attending Alpha classes with her church before we married in 2010. I often say that thanks to God and Lee-Ann. At the end of 2009, when I turned thirty, I became a man.

Our honeymoon was to Niagara Falls because it only cost a couple of hundred bucks on the Canadian side. Including the wedding event, dress, and rings, the entire wedding cost five grand, which wouldn't have purchased a single plate at an Italian wedding like the one our Executive Director Daniel Prete threw. The ring has little black spots on the diamond, and I've always wanted to upgrade or replace the ring. Lee-Ann always rejects the offer, saying, "never, I'd rather give that money away to charity. This ring is perfect and there will never be another one like it." That woman slays me and she isn't even trying. She has absolutely no shopping budget for herself, I even tried to get her to buy a luxury sports car recently, but she refuses.

"I'll tell you what, Jamie. I'll take the three thousand a month you spend on your McLaren and invest it into something that brings me real joy." I got so excited! I could see my wife pulling up in a Lambo or a convertible Porsche with her blond hair windblown on a summer's day. Before I could go any further with my car/wife fantasy she said, "I'm going to take that money and give it away to people in our church and community who need it. I already know somebody who needs to fly home to see her sick mom. I'll buy her tickets this afternoon." And that's how it is with Lee-Ann. In the sweetest way, she's a shark. She's the quintessential badass. Lee-Ann and I had our youngest child, Takiyah, together in 2011, exactly nine months after we got married, and not a week earlier, *Mom.*

We're a blended family, with my biological daughter Haylee, who's 21; Lee-Ann's biological son Addison, who's 20 and calls me dad; my biological son Hayden, who's 19; and of course, Takiyah, who's 10.

When Lee-Ann and I had Takiyah, we'd already learned a lot from the ten years prior when we'd had our first children. Back then, we'd bought into the ideas of people who said "don't worry about your kids when they're small, they'll really need you when they're teenagers." But by the time Haylee, Addison and Hayden were teenagers, they knew dad as a workaholic, not as a loving, protecting father. I'd slaved away in my former company, and they really didn't even know me. Lee-Ann and I worked eighty-hour weeks back then.

When we built Experior, Takiyah was still a toddler. Among so many progressive things we've done at Experior, we set out to discover how you could build a business and still put your family first. At our last meeting with the six-figure earners that we call Executive Directors with Experior, I loved to see how many men and women had young children crawling up their arms and sticking their faces in front of the camera on Zoom. I take screenshots in those moments and text them to Lee-Ann. #FamilyFirst, I will write. She responds with a heart emoji. We did it.

Lee-Ann is the most empathetic creature in existence. She would probably be happy to have no money because she'd have given it all away. This is a way we temper and learn from one another daily. She has her Bless Me Fund, the first beneficiary of which was the woman I mentioned who needed a flight to see her aging, ill mother. She once gave a guy in our company a bunch of money when he was in some challenging straits, and come to think of it, the only time I find that she excessively spends money is at the grocery store. She responds, "I always make sure everyone has enough."

Counterintuitively, this empathy is what makes her so wealthy. She understands that the more money we make, the more we can give away – It's like a Robin Hood operation. Before we were even dating, I later found out that she had anonymously paid my rent for me. I had told her that my landlord hadn't asked for the money yet, and it had already been three days since it was due. After me stressing over the rent being due and not hearing from the Landlord, she told me someone probably paid it for me. It didn't take long before I realized it was her. The crazy thing is that she was just as broke as me at that time. The woman is all heart, I tell ya! At that time she didn't even know I was planning to make a move on her romantically; she just wanted to bring me to the Lord. Thankfully I'm a great closer, so I got her, even though I was as broke as a joke.

One of Lee-Ann's many talents is intuition; were it not for her I would have lost many more millions than I have with all of the sleazeballs there are in the industry. You see, Lee-Ann smells bullshit from a mile away. Ten years ago, when we left our Practice Company and decided to go into business for ourselves, Lee-Ann and I started our own agency. Six months later, after achieving some mild success, we were approached by and decided to partner with three gentlemen who promised us the moon and the stars.

"We have the systems built; you just bring us the agents." Lee-Ann saw the fraud coming and one day said, "We're working ten-hour days and these guys show up at 10 a.m. and leave after lunch... this isn't sustainable, Jamie."

After fifteen months of building these guys' company for them, we told them we wanted our company back.

"That's not how this works, this isn't your company anymore," they replied, and just like that, we had worked ten years in our previous company and two years in our new company, but in December of 2013, we were penniless again.

In kind fashion with the cutthroat insurance industry, these guys then went behind our backs and tried to discredit us with insurance carriers, to the point where I was ready to throw punches when one of them wouldn't give me a contract. Thankfully, Lee-Ann held me back, on one of the rare times I needed her to, and I held my cool. Darren Golka is known to say that, behind-the-scenes, Lee-Ann puts me in my place. I can neither confirm nor deny that suspicion, but I'm happy to say that recently, that same guy with whom we'd fought with to get a contract said, "Every time you tell me what you're doing for the year I roll my eyes... and then you do even more." That company is now one of our major partners here in Canada. They once said in an f-bomb war that if I didn't hit numbers, he'd cut my contract, now we do more volume in a week than we used to do in a year with our ex-partners previously.

Lee-Ann and I have now been in this industry for a combined thirty-five years, but it's only in the last eight that we've gone from a negative net worth to building a $50 million company that's exploding in growth every year. When we set out to build the UFC (Ultimate Financial Company), there were moments when we would butt heads. I think about sales whereas Lee-Ann is passionate about the personnel. Before the pandemic, she provided lunch for our employees every day, which speaks for itself. She's the President of our company, overseeing staff, hiring, firing, and running departments. When we've had disagreements in our business in the past, Lee-Ann has said several times that I'm the man in the family so she's leaving the decision with me. I think that it's code for, "Look out! We are probably better off doing it my way."

Chapter Two Lessons:

#1. A great woman isn't behind every great man, but she is beside him.

#2. The more money you make, the more people you can bless.

Chapter Three

Positively Brainwashed

"There's a compounding effect when you don't give up."
Tzachi Chen, Experior Executive Director

"It's not how you start; it's how you stay."
Jamie Prickett

How would you feel if I gave you a million dollars, no strings attached? Now, what if I told you that I would bump that up to ten million? But here's the caveat: you will not wake up tomorrow.

Would you still take the ten million if you knew that you'd cease to exist tomorrow morning? Absolutely not! The ten million dollars would be worthless. You wouldn't take it. You value your life more than ten million dollars.

So why don't you wake up every day feeling like a million bucks if you value your life more than ten million dollars?

I refer to our agents at Experior as kings and queens. Nothing tears me up more than reading the stories of other founders and startup companies, and how much they put on the line before achieving success. It's no wonder that common entrepreneur memes include references to a lack of sleep, exhaustion, and the concept that we're downright crazy. We've slain some raging mad dragons to bring Experior Financial Group to fruition, and along the way, we partnered up with some warriors such as Team

FML, Team REOS, Rainmakers Leadership Alliance (Ryan & Corinne Tongs' organization), The Legacy Builders (Baljit & Pam Parmar's organization), SEAL Team (Francis & Dianne Sinday's organization) and today we're expanding rapidly with American organizations, such as Team Wealth Makers, spearheaded by husband and wife team leaders Raza and Imrana Begg, and so many more!

Team FML originally referred to Frank, Mauro, and Laval, but became affectionately known as Team FML for their slogan: Free More Lives. The FML team joined Experior in 2016. Team REOS joined us two years later, in 2018, led by Darren and Stephanie Golka and their longtime friend and former business colleague, Bhupinder Cheema. REOS stands for: Recognize Each Other's Success.

From Left to Right: Frank De Lio, Laval Dubeau, and Mauro Arturi
Team "Free More Lives"

The road to success with Experior wasn't pathed in gold. In fact, it wasn't pathed at all. It's been more of a slog through the jungle with dull machetes. But every time we encountered a new menacing snake (there were many) or a rodent of unusual size (a lot of financial services bad habits and poor models that we're changing), Lee-Ann and I have been diligent in remembering this phrase: *you can change your life in a single breath, but you must decide.*

In a single breath, you can make a decision; you can decide to win. The word decision comes from Latin. The suffix *cide* means "killing." With deCIDE, you make a decision to "kill off" any other alternatives. Also, think homicide, suicide, or pesticide. In a breath, you can manifest your perfect future, even if it takes time to materialize. I tell my team that when you make a decision, you are effectively killing off all other options than the option to win.

I already mentioned in Chapter One that Lee-Ann and I don't come from money or privilege. Considering she's a high school dropout and it took me five years to graduate by the skin of my teeth, we don't have any special MIT-level talents that make us stereotypically fit to have built an industry-disrupting financial services agency. What we do have is mindset, and some might say that we are "positively brainwashed."

The term positively brainwashed has been used by my agents as a double entendre. It illustrates both my own positive insanity at times and also supports the fact that I'm leading what we affectionately call "a personal development program with a great compensation package." Authentic, genuine, honest mindset training is a core component of our agents' success. It is far more important than financial degrees or even industry experience, your team will go miles further with a mindset core competency over a standard skillset, and you'll be wise to remember that in your hiring and recruiting efforts.

I also believe that the industry that I am in is not for everyone but could be for anyone. Sometimes, people don't know until they try. My goal is that if someone pursues a different career path after a stint with Experior, they can walk away knowing that they have grown as a person. Our dream wasn't to just make people rich. Our dream was to show people how to be successful leaders in their businesses as well as their communities, places of worship, relationships with their spouses, children, and so on.

Lee-Ann and I are the proverbial underdogs, but we implore you to commit this critical life lesson to memory right now: *if we can do it, so can you.* It won't be easy. We're rule-benders, mold-shatterers, and the hardest working couple you'll ever meet. Some of my agents even argue that Lee-Ann is the real workhorse because she spends a bit more time doing and a bit less time talking than me.

If you're a positively-brainwashed, extroverted, rally-the-troops dynamic sales and marketing type of person, I can't express enough the value of having a humble, systems-oriented, behind-the-scenes partner in your business. If you're a brilliant behind-the-scenes mechanic or process-oriented person, I also can't express the immeasurable value of having a dynamic face to sell your business and magnify your presence in the world. Lee-Ann and I truly are the perfectly balanced contrast.

I'm not sure that the humble beginnings, such as Lee-Ann and I have had, are necessarily critical to your success, but what those humble beginnings begat was *hunger. Failure has never been an option.* Your success is predicated on that hunger. We didn't have a leg up on you. We're no better than you, no matter where you are.

With the right mindset, you're one breath away from your next win.

Maybe you've lived, or are still living, paycheck-to-paycheck. Maybe you walked out of your last job without notice because you worried that if you didn't get out of there, somebody was going down... and maybe that somebody was you. Maybe you dream of buying a house or stocking money away for retirement while you're still young enough to enjoy it. Maybe you dream of a trip to Europe, not just in a lifetime, but every year. Maybe you have feared that without a trust fund or nepotism, it's not possible to get ahead in life; your only option is to be a slave to a 9-to-5 job, clocking in and out of some soulless, whitewashed cubicle, and that scares the crap out of you. Maybe you're like Lee-Ann and me; you're an underdog. And to you, I say: don't stop. Don't give up. Ever.

The successful agents you'll read about in this book chose to prove the haters wrong. They put blinders on to the criticism, berating, and bullying. Maybe haters have made fun of you for your grades, your sports performances, your clothes, hell, they made fun of your mom.

Maybe, worst of all, that hater is in your head. Those negative thoughts are the enemy. Those negative thoughts are the haters. If you're somebody who wants to put those haters in their place - me too - we have something in common. Rest assured that, over the course of this book, we'll tackle some of those negative thoughts in an unprecedented way, without all the ooey-gooey psychobabble and fluff. We're going to make a great team.

You will remember from Chapter One that I loved wrestling as a kid. I wrestled well into my twenties and even took home some awards, even after my first marriage ended. This happened despite having almost no recent training, being slightly above my preferred weight class, and having spent a few too many hours drinking away my sorrows at the broken home I had. Wrestling was my first addiction, and in so many ways it's like the addiction I have now: to fight a worthy opponent and win. Wrestling, to me, was going to be my ticket out of the seemingly inevitable fate of being a loser. So I did it, and I did it well.

As I mentioned earlier, in high school I graduated by the skin of my teeth with a D+ average; 59% to be exact, and even that took me five years. On the very morning that Lee-Ann and I told our upline that we were quitting at the Practice Company on September 9, 2011, our ten-year-old son Addison was rushed to the hospital with kidney failure. Only two people from a company I'd worked with for ten years showed up in the hospital; one was a lady from our church and the other was a woman who now works with us at Experior.

I'll never forget that afternoon, rushing to Hamilton Sick Kids Hospital where our boy was in the ICU. Thoughts of neglecting my children raced through my head. Leaving the Practice Company where Lee-Ann and I had met was my attempt to right some wrongs... a lot of them.

"We're not sure whether or not he's going to make it out of here... Mrs. Prickett," the doctor said to my wife a couple of weeks into the ordeal at the hospital. Lee-Ann showed emotion. But me? I was paralyzed with grief and humiliation. I couldn't heal his kidneys, but I could have given Addison a better life. I knew that when he got out, if he got out, I'd be around a hell of a lot more.

Over the ten years that I was with the Practice Company, the last two of which I was honored to be Addison's step-dad, I worked ding-to-dong, seven days a week, for the entire decade. The only way I knew how to unwind was to drink in the evenings, that is until Lee-Ann and the Lord smartened me up! Even today, I lament having listened to my upline when they said that ridiculous phrase about how children don't need you when they're small, just when they're teenagers. By the time my children were teenagers, it was too late. One fell into serious drug addiction. Another dropped out of high school and has been in trouble with the law, and Addison still struggles every day with rejection medication and a constant feeling that he explains is similar to having the flu. Thank God, as of late, they are both doing much better.

If you take just one more critical life lesson away from my story, remember this: your children love you. They're wired to love you. They need you. They want your attention. They need your loving reprimand. They need discipline. They're not psychologically equipped to "figure it out on their own." You will never, ever get the time back with them when they're small. I pray you won't be like me and piss that time away for a company that ultimately leaves you destitute.

On Literally the same day that Addison was in transit to the hospital, my upline at the Practice Company made it to my office and removed all of my branch files. He could have waited a few days, as I had no intention at that time to even stay in the industry, but I suppose he was motivated by fear.

Returning from the ICU with Lee-Ann and Addison a month later to that empty office reminded me of the heartless place I'd worked at and the void left in my children's lives. For ten years this gentleman had been like a brother to me. I envisioned that we'd still hang out on the weekends once in a while. But no. I was no longer an asset to him. I vowed that going forward, I would live, love, lead my staff and team, and parent, with compassion and respect. In that first month when Addison was in critical care, not once did my upline come to visit. That neglect fueled anger in me and planted the seed that maybe, just maybe, I would stay in the industry, just to do it better. Prior to this disappointment, my commitment to my upline would never have allowed me to feel good about working with a competing company, let alone building one eventually. I guess this is the silver lining in that story.

Today, Addison works with Experior two to three days a week. The rest of the time, he's too sick to leave the house. He'll most likely live with us for a very long time, if not forever. We've found a place for him, though; he handles some marketing and has a keen eye for graphic design.

Today, Lee-Ann and I have Takiyah, our ten-year-old daughter at the time of my writing this book. Takiyah doesn't know the life her older siblings endured. She doesn't know a dad who isn't there. She doesn't know what it's like to hear Mom and Dad have "swearing fights." The worst she'll ever hear is some sarcastic comments and arguments that more resemble business negotiations. She'll never know what it's like to go to a restaurant and order the starchiest, most filling thing on the menu because we can't waste money on empty calories like vegetables, salads, fruit bowls, or salsas.

After our scare with Addison and the sobering realization that I was at rock-bottom in life, things actually got a helluva lot worse.

For six months following our resignation from the Practice Company, Lee-Ann and I started selling insurance independently. We couldn't believe how much more income we were immediately able to earn. Another six months later, we started a company called Empirical Group together, just the two of us. Alas, we were still in the industry and working like slaves, but we were independent. We didn't feel like we had to beg people to sell a dream to others while we were living a nightmare in order to recruit them.

After six months building Empirical Group, our new "baby," we were approached by three guys who looked to have a valuable company... on paper. The problem was that we didn't know that they were laaaaaazy; they'd have us doing all of the work while they sat back and collected paychecks.

It started innocently enough, and like many people I have encountered over the years in business negotiations, they promised us the sun and the moon. They were impressive enough (at least to me, Lee-Ann always had her reservations), so we ended up with 25% ownership in the companies that we merged, and a seventy-five split between our new partners. At the time, it wasn't a big company, but we were cranking around $75,000 a month in insurance premiums, which was more than I'd ever done in ten years with the Practice Company. Lee-Ann and I began to make $20-25,000 a month, and we thought things were going pretty well.

That is, until Christmastime 2013. I called a meeting with our three partners, which was a struggle to organize considering they only worked four hours a day or less. I told them that we weren't happy with the two of us working more in a single day than the three of them worked in an entire week. The infrastructure that we'd set up wasn't designed in our favor; we were aware that we'd been played. After a few choice words I had with them, and then Lee-Ann jumping in on the verbal war (I was so proud of her for standing on guard), they asked us to give them a few days to see what they could work out.

Well, they sure tried to work something out, alright. Two days before Christmas they sent us an email. In that email, they laid out three offers. Each one of the offers actually made things worse for Lee-Ann and me, not better. That was eight years ago. I didn't just cry about it. I experienced the first glimpse of depression I'd ever felt in my life. I'm usually the most upbeat, friendly, downright boisterous, and bellowing voice in the room, no doubt about that. But that year I was paralyzed. Reading that email, my stomach turned as I wondered, "How can I start over... again?"

That night, Lee-Ann and I were standing in our bedroom. I could barely take off my clothes so I sprawled across the bed, staring at the ceiling, motionless. I heard my wife's sweet voice gently say, "Maybe God's got a bigger plan. And He hasn't shown us yet." I knew that she was right, even though I didn't want to hear it.

I felt completely defeated; this was an emotion that I had never felt before. Thank God it only lasted for about a week! During that time, I read the biography of somebody who went through much worse than I was facing at that moment. Still, I was angry - really angry. With the business partners screwing us, people who were like family to me at the Practice Company were so brainwashed that they thought we had become overnight criminals because we were now working at a competing company.

Lee-Ann's words sunk in over the coming weeks and I regained my courage... and composure.

About a week after the holidays, I posted the only negative thing I've ever posted on Facebook in my entire life:

> Just took the worst 'low blow' of my entire life in business! I thought 3 weeks ago was bad, but tonight took the cake. BUT I'm still smiling. ☺ I AM blessed to have a mighty powerful God who can use all things for good and a super, awesome, sexy, strong, bold, courageous, woman of God, Lee-Ann Bailey Prickett. This 'set back' is nothing more than a 'set up' for bigger and better things to come!! The future is brighter than ever (Shhhh... :)). Sometimes God will bring us the greatest blessings at the lowest moments in our lives... and some of the amazing people around me have proven this to be true!!! #2Blessed2Bstressed #strongerthanever

That week I called up my friend Joe from one of the insurance carriers we had been doing business with and said, "Joe, we need an MGA contract. I'm leaving my partners and I need to be an MGA direct with you, just like we are now." (If you're unfamiliar with insurance-speak, an MGA, or Managing General Agent, is a contract between an insurance company and an agency, to have the ability to recruit agents to offer their products.)

"Well, Jamie. I can't do that."

"What are you talking about, brother? We built Empirical in two years. We're the only reason these three guys have a company doing any business. Why won't you give us a contract?" I didn't tell him that Lee-Ann and I were penniless.

"Jamie, they're the ones with the relationship, and we can't give you a contract."

"Joe, they won't survive without me. Lee-Ann and I are the only reason they're doing any business right now." F-bombs ensued.

Finally, Joe relented, "Fine, Jamie. I'll give you the blankety-blank contract, but if you screw this up, I'm pulling it at the end of this year."

"Let's do it." And so we received our contract, and on January 22, 2014, Experior was born.

Chapter Three Lessons:

#1: With the right mindset, you're one breath away from your next win.

#2: Your children don't just need you in the future, they need you now.

#3: Allow your anger to water the seeds of change; let the bad times fuel your desire to create a better life.

Chapter Four

It's Darkest Before Dawn

"I love changing lives, but, selfishly, I love a good fight, too."
Jamie Prickett

"Easy and elite were never meant to coexist. Throughout history, elite high performers didn't escape suffering - they embraced it. By carrying their cross, they discovered the crown."
Tom Ryan, Head Coach of the OSU National Championship Wrestling Team

While I was writing this book, I got a call from good old Joe.

He said, "Hey Jamie, here are your numbers for the year so far. Man, you're freakin' killin' it again."

"Thanks, man. Thanks for believing in us. We're still so grateful."

"Seriously, Jamie. It's shocking. I can't believe it, but just when I think you guys have capped out and you're setting a ridiculous goal yet again, by the end of that year I'm rolling my eyes saying 'holy crap, they did it again.'" This is the same guy from Chapter Three who, eight years earlier, almost didn't give us a contract because our ex-partners tried to have us blocked. Unfortunately, this is just some of the back-stabbing and vicious behavior that is frankly commonplace in our industry.

Maybe it's commonplace in every industry. But remember, if you aren't a threat, they're not going to talk about you. They're not going to say, "Jamie's a raging lunatic and he's going to run that company into the ground" unless you pose a threat. We started Experior fueled by a combination of wanting (not needing) to prove our haters wrong and desperation. One year later... well... that was the year we couldn't pay our taxes and had to borrow $5,000 from my mother-in-law.

And the setbacks didn't cease for us.

Two years into building Experior, shortly after the FML warriors joined forces with us, I'm sitting in my office with a stack of contracts piled next to me, looking at a late night... possibly working until two a.m. Experior was still a relatively new company and Lee-Ann and I were, once again, working around the clock to build it up. My eyes are dry. Every time I blink, my eyelids stick to my eyeballs and threaten to scratch my corneas. I kick open the door to our fridge. Not an iced coffee or energy drink in sight, so I settle for the bottle of water that I keep on hand for clients. I glance at the wastebasket in the corner. There must be twenty coffee cups in there. I determine that I'm just a bit dehydrated, take a swig, set the water bottle on my desk, and decide to walk out to the front reception area of the office we moved into shortly after our flower shop office. I remember Rochelle, who has played just about every Head Office admin role for us at that point, saying, "Jamie, you have a big package that just arrived from FedEx."

I take it back to my office to open it up and it is two large binders. I'll never forget that moment. The words blurred a bit. My hands went numb. I blinked slowly and begged my heart to keep beating; it was stuck in my throat. Those binders revealed to me that we were being sued by one of the largest financial services companies in North America, the Practice Company. *David versus Goliath.*

In the financial industry, some companies have a non-solicitation clause, indicating that you can't solicit any of your clients for two years. I think this is complete BS since agents are the ones who develop their own clientele, many times starting off with friends, families, and acquaintances. The lawsuit accused Frank De Lio, Mauro Arturi, and Laval Dubeau of violations of their non-solicitation agreements. It also accused Experior of using trade secrets to recruit people (I didn't know it was such a secret that we were just more awesome than them). In the forty-odd years since that company was founded, we were the exponents of the biggest raid their company had ever experienced by a competitor in Canada. They were intent on making a public spectacle of our hanging to threaten others. If it were medieval Rome or during Biblical times, we'd have been nailed to a cross or stoned in the middle of the piazza.

The most frustrating part was that we were merely being targeted as we posed a threat, and not because of the validity of their claims. Over ten years I had represented that company with pride, honor, and ethics. Not one blemish existed on my record. But now, four years after leaving them and two years into building Experior, they started a war with us.

To add insult to injury, our biggest team, one that had been doing $100,000 a month in premium prior to this debacle, quit as a result of that lawsuit. They told everyone that Experior was doomed, that we were going out of business. They scavenged people we'd brought into Experior, but we rolled up our sleeves and prepared ourselves for a fight.

Even my old upline in the Practice Company, a man who was at our wedding and was like a brother to me, said, "We're going to crush Experior," not thinking about my wife, my family, or my agents. I thought that dealing with betrayal and haters was bad... but it was soon going to get much worse.

Look, Frank, Mauro, and Laval or Team FML, always thought I was nuts. Bonkers, in fact. Mauro says that when he first saw me speak, he thought I was bat-shit crazy, but those men stood with me through that fight. They believed in me, in Lee-Ann, and in Experior.

Once I finally gathered the courage to read the contents of those two binders, I recalled the words of my high school wrestling coach Frank Corning. He'd say, "Jamie, you need to eat, sleep and shit wrestling. You want to win? You gotta suck it up, Prickett."

I thought about Doug Cox, a three-time Olympian and one of my wrestling coaches after I graduated from high school. He'd say, "I'd rather have a wrestler who doesn't have talent but gives it their all."

I thought about Dave Mair, a coach of mine after high school who had a take no prisoners approach to the sport. If he ever caught me taking a breather during practice, or laying on the mat after a hard scrimmage, he'd say, "Get up, Prickett! Do you think your opponent cares how tired you are?" To this day, I have a tremendous amount of gratitude to Mair for teaching me to be tough.

Over the next six months, paying two attorneys $1,000+ an hour for a crime we didn't commit was shattering, but there was never a moment that I felt like giving up. Sure, I woke up pissed off for 180 days straight, but it wasn't depression. It was anger. I told myself that it wasn't going to have ill effects on my health. I kept visualizing my why and my purpose: to not only fight this company that was suing us but to fight an entire industry that was full of broken promises, thieving companies, and false hopes. And in that vision of rewriting this entire industry, I found immense hope.

It would have been easy to pack our bags and go home. Maybe bankrupt the company and go get a job. In fact, there was a moment when the Practice Company's lawyer handed over papers with a large settlement number and a lengthy non-compete.

"They're going to try and sink you guys," our lawyer said coldly and matter-of-factly. I didn't blink an eye. I ripped the paper to shreds right in front of them. Mauro, Laval, and Frank didn't so much as twitch. They didn't look happy, but they weren't surprised either. At that moment, they were either scared of me or they respected me. To this day I'm not certain. So, we kept fighting... and sometimes we even found ways to make it fun. But mostly, it sucked.

Laval Dubeau remembers sitting in the high-rise of the Toronto office building where our attorneys were soon to arrive. He nodded his head towards a table with pastries, drinks, and other treats. I nodded back and we made our way over to the table, stuffing our plates with breakfast before the attorneys arrived in the office. We must have looked guilty because when they abruptly entered the conference room one of them said, "Go ahead and have your fill. Those Sprites cost about $5 each, but you're paying for it." I looked over at Laval and he read my mind. "Cheers, man," I said as I twisted the cap on my soda to prepare for another brutal meeting.

We've had some tough times: I already told you about how our son's kidney failed in 2011 right when we left the Practice Company; one of our children had some substance abuse issues; I've been divorced, as has Lee-Ann; and we didn't pay taxes our first year in business at Experior.

But nothing stings like being accused of something you didn't do by a company that was worth over $7 billion at the time they sued us. Like the cheese Danishes and $5 Sprite episode; the attorneys didn't care about us. Remember, they were billing us at $1,000+ an hour to listen to us talk. They knew we were being made examples of, that we were being exploited because we were a threat. That really soured me on attorneys, to be honest. Anybody with enough money can file accusations against another individual, who then has to come up with enough money to clear their name, even if they were innocent all along, hence the anger I woke up with every morning for 180 days straight.

What does a wrestler do with anger? He lifts heavy weights until he pukes. To manage that anger, I started immediately seeing a personal trainer, Matt Daciw. Matt is an embarrassingly beautiful man and is totally jacked. Ironically, he used to be with the insurance company that was suing me. Through a combination of empathy and rigorous drilling, Matt helped me reconnect with my fire and light when everything else threatened to dim it. He became my veritable therapist during those months.

There were a few sunny moments during this circus of a legal battle, such as the handful of times that representatives from the Practice Company flew all the way from Georgia, U.S.A. to Toronto, Ontario with a handful of lawyers. We knew the Practice Company must have been paying each one of these suits at least fifteen hundred bucks an hour. At one point, the Practice Company's lawyers said, "We honestly can't believe you're putting up a fight. We're *all* bleeding money." To hear that the other side was suffering too was music to my ears. I knew I had a chance; we were exhausting our opponent. Goliath was getting tired, lazy, and sloppy...

The lawsuit ended around the Canadian Thanksgiving time in late October. Frank De Lio, Mauro Arturi, and Laval Dubeau, along with their respective wives, Yolanda, Mara, and Natalie, presented Lee-Ann and me with a signed picture of UFC Champion George St. Pierre fighting.

"For the man who will never, ever give up," Laval said. I'll never remove that photo from my office. It's right behind my desk so that everybody can see it on Zoom. I'm not just a CEO, I'm a fighter, or as Experior Executive Director, Madhab Dulal says to this day, "We're warriors with the intention to rebuild an entire industry with integrity."

FML Leaders and their wives presenting me with the George St. Pierre signed picture (left to right) Natalie Dubeau, Mara Arturi, Yolanda De Lio, Lee-Ann Prickett, Jamie Prickett, Laval Dubeau, Frank De Lio, Mauro Arturi

Just four months after the lawsuit ended, we rented a community center for our first Experior annual convention. We ran out of food. It was embarrassing, but I remained as enthusiastic as if I was in the Grand Ballroom of the Ritz Hotel, just like that time in our first Experior office above the flower shop. Laval remembers walking into this rec room in the middle of the boonies thinking, "This is it? This is what we've been fighting the Goliath for?" But Laval and Natalie stood with us, and they still stand with us today.

The fight with the Practice Company became our greatest asset; being David facing Goliath shaped and chastened our team (me, Lee-Ann, and Team FML) into even more fearless leaders.

We didn't just fight a $7 billion company that year. We fought for every one of our now 1,700 agents and the progressive, mold-shattering company we were building... for them.

The total cost of the lawsuit would end up being $375,000, 200,000 of which was the responsibility of Lee-Ann and myself to pay, and the three FML studs paid the remainder. That hurt back then for all of us, but today, that's chump change for Experior or any member of the five of us in the lawsuit. We kept our licenses, we weren't found guilty, and despite the setbacks and the loss of agents during the suit, I wouldn't change it for the world! It truly helped us continue to look at our model and how to improve it. We learned to work smarter, not just harder.

At the time of the lawsuit, I was still a bit of a wild card. The team didn't love me all the time, but they loved what we were creating. Today, those men are my brothers.

Chapter Four Lessons:

#1: In a David versus Goliath fight, visualize your why and your purpose. Remember that you aren't fighting a single monster, but an entire legion of bad guys or, in our case, an entire industry full of broken promises, thieving companies, and false hope. If you're gonna fight, fight them all.

#2. Goliath will get lazy, sloppy, and vulnerable. Stay aware and look for your chance to strike if, by nothing else, then with your ability to never quit.

Chapter Five

The Precise Model That Disrupted The Entire Insurance Industry

"Jamie will change anything if it's in service to his agents."
Mauro Arturi, Executive Director at Experior and the "M" in Team FML

"We're here to change a bloated, cutthroat, corrupt industry."
Henok Msghina, Experior Executive Director

Speaking at an Experior Convention

How did Lee-Ann and I go from a couple of exhausted agents with nothing in the bank account to a company with over 1,700 agents worth $50 million? There are over 400 Managing General Agencies (MGAs) in Canada alone, so why is Experior rapidly becoming number one? How did we become the first, and currently only, Independent Marketing Organization (IMO) in Canadian history to expand into the U.S.A.? (By the way, MGA is a Canadian term, while IMO is an American term. Same industry.)

If you're like most people, you tuned out the images of my crappy car woes and focused on the nice house with the indoor swimming pool. You're flipping pages looking for the formula to get you from your current life to... well... Lee-Ann's and mine, in 30 days or less. I think that's great, actually. You deserve everything you want and more, and you're probably reading because you want to know what we did so that you can duplicate that formula in your own life. That's smart, and I commend you. We all learn by standing on the shoulders of giants. Not a day goes by that I don't consume books or training from great leaders that have gone before me.

I also know that all my haters have skipped ahead to this chapter because you're wondering: "How the hell did that clown do it?" And to that, I say, "Eat your heart out."

A word of warning: if you're reading this book as an entrepreneur or intrapreneur who's interested in our meteoric rise to becoming a successful company, Chapter Five will dive deep into the specific models relevant to the insurance industry. If you're looking for the non-insurance-related leadership and business greatness models that we've used to scale our business from zero to $50 million, skip this chapter and head to Part Two now.

The Tribrid Model

Experior has disrupted the insurance industry for good with something we call "The Tribrid Model." The Tribrid Model is a combination of the three more prominent models from the

Canadian financial advising and insurance industry rolled up into one system that allows everybody to win: from agents to agency builders, and all the way to the clients.

If you're American, don't stop reading. As of early 2021, we licensed our first IMO agent in the United States; a feat that was thus far unprecedented by any other Canadian company. IMO stands for Independent Marketing Organization: an organization that works with insurance companies to market their products. By the time this book reaches your hands, we'll likely have agents in all 50 U.S. States. If you're trapped in a system where you feel like the entire thing is rigged for the old dogs or the founders to win, or where you're not earning your worth and where you don't own your clientele or agency, head over to YouTube and watch this earth-shattering description of how we've disrupted the entire industry: These links will take you there:

www.ExperiorUSAVideo.com
www.ExperiorCANADAVideo.com

People are generally familiar with three primary models in the insurance brokerage world.

1. The first model is the **Independent Model, or IMO/MGA**. In this model, brokers chase the highest compensation for the products they sell. They're focused on the highest rate they can get paid for products. From the perspective of a salesperson, it makes perfect sense to want to make the most commission for the products that you're selling. In addition, you will typically have access to different companies or carriers - sometimes over 100 different carriers to find the product that best suits their client's unique needs. I've found that the IMO/MGA offers the most benefits for agents on compensation and because of the flexibility of finding the product that gets

your client from point A to point B, regardless of his or her life situation, health, or financial means. Because of their appeal, many companies disguise themselves as IMOs when they're really just pure network marketing or MLM companies.

2. The second model is an **MLM (Multi-Level Marketing)/Networking Marketing or Builder's Model**. Agents can recruit other agents in their downline as well as work part-time around their schedules. I know it sounds odd to associate insurance agencies and financial brokerages with network marketing, which one generally associates low-ticket products like pills, potions, lotions, makeup, cleaning products, or even clothes. But believe it or not, this has been a common practice among insurance agencies for decades. The issue with these models is that if you don't get in early, it may be difficult, or near impossible, to make a great living. The compensation is extremely low for the agents that are actually making the sales, while the whales collect most of the revenue.
3. The third model is the **Captive Agency Model.** Most captive agencies offer incredible training and support to their agents. Some of these companies are great companies that will show you the ropes, so to speak. Some of the challenges arise around client options, as many of these agents are not able to "broker" out better solutions for their clients if needed.

A Word of Warning Regarding MLMs or Network Marketing Companies

As you've read, there are outliers and unicorns; a handful of representatives in the Producer or Builder Models who have great success. However, you find that statistically, a vast majority of representatives in these models struggle to get by. Later on, you'll read about several dozen of my Executive Directors who struggled for 5, 10, or even 20 years to get to where Experior brought them in as little as six months. You'll read about men and women who were in a Builder's Model industry, recognized by their companies as "Presidents" and "Vice Presidents," who couldn't pay their bills. I was one of them.

Innocent men and women everywhere join MLMs with hopes of joining a team model wherein they are incentivized to recruit a "downline" team whilst selling the company's product, which could be literally anything. Although the MLMs are generally packaged as low-investment opportunities for anything from a busy corporate executive looking to earn cash through a "side hustle" and, most tragically, to mothers who need to work from home, and that between incentives, products, phone, internet, giveaways, computer supplies, advertising, monthly training products, conferences, and travel, MLM participants in most cases spend more money than they actually earn. Again, there are outliers, but this holds true for most.

I'm all about investing in one's business. Nice clothes, a fast computer, traveling to have face-to-face time with clients and teammates, and attending conventions are valuable investments I encourage everybody on my team to make. But in the MLM Models, do they provide enough ROI to justify the expense? Traditionally, no. The AARP Foundation found that only 25% of MLM participants profited from their upfront investments in MLM companies. 27% broke even, and nearly half of them lost money. For the 25% who profited, 14% made less than $5,000 (USD), 6% made between $5,000-$9,999, 3% made between $10,000-$24,999, 3% made $25,000 or more, and just a half a percent made $100,000 or more[1].

1 AARP Foundation Infographic. "AARP Study of Multilevel Marketing: Profiling Participants and Their Experiences in Direct Sales," https://centerforinquiry.org/wp-content/uploads/sites/33/quackwatch/taylor.pdf. Pages 8-9, 13. Accessed March 23, 2021.

The AARP Foundation found that 44% of participants in MLMs dropped out after just a year[2], 90% dropped out within five years, and nearly every single soul who entered an MLM filled with hopes of being the next million-dollar producer dropped out by year ten.

Houston, we have a problem.

And if your wife is as intelligent, driven, and heart-centered as mine, you would have done exactly what we've done.

Enter: The Tribrid Model.

Builder's Model + Career Model + IMO/MGO Model

To further break these down we can categorize the MLM/Network Marketing as the BUILDER'S MODEL, and the IMO/MGA and Captive Models as the PERSONAL PRODUCER MODELS:

2 AARP Foundation. "AARP Study of Multilevel Marketing: Profiling Participants and Their Experiences in Direct Sales," https://www.aarp.org/content/dam/aarp/aarp_foundation/2018/pdf/AARP%20Foundation%20MLM%20Research%20Study%20Report%2010.8.18.pdf. Page 5. Accessed March 23, 2021.

Builder's Model Vs. Personal Producer Models

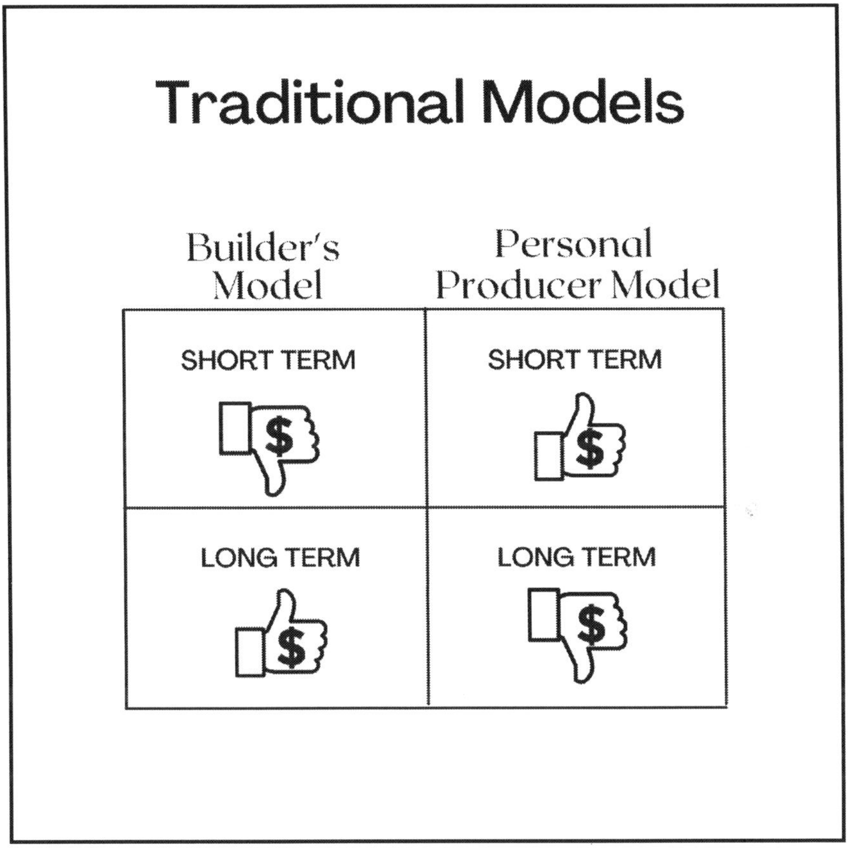

#1: The Builder's Model

Benefit: The Builder's Model is exceptional and exciting. Agents have the ability to recruit others and build a team of producers who write business under the original agent or upline. This allows the recruiting agent to build exponential passive income. The other benefit is that agents can, after many years or decades, retire or go part-time in their business while still bringing in income.

Problem: This model tends to have low rates of compensation, which is why I often say that most people end up starving their way to try and reach the top. Some people make a lot of money if they get in early, but by the time most people even hear about the opportunity, it has pretty much passed them by.

#2: Personal Producer's Model

Benefit: In the short term, the personal producer can earn great compensation.

Problem: However, because the personal producer doesn't have a downline, once he or she retires or goes part-time, the income dwindles. In the insurance industry, agents don't have pensions. Another problem with the Personal Producer Model is something called burnout. When you burnout in this particular model, your income dies in direct correlation with your reduced hours. Most agents will have to sell for 20, 30, or even 40 years and still won't generate the amount of residual income they were earning while they were actively selling.

Builder Model Problem: SOLVED

Our agents have the opportunity to recruit into their downline as well as receive generous compensation for personal production. Agents like Andrea Rogers, Mauro Arturi, Tzachi Chen, Frank De Lio, and Darren Golka prefer to lead their teams and take very few personal clients. They're dominating the Builder's Model by building teams from which they receive override compensation. Rather than write individual business, they serve as coaches and team leaders to the agents working with the end-user.

Personal Producer Problem: SOLVED

Agents who love working with individual clients on financial education, such as Mark Ferland, Dror David, Daniel Prete, Matthew Stewart, Henok Mgshina, Madhab Dulal, and Tariq Ba'Aqeel, are free to spend all the time they want nurturing their clients and serving primarily as true financial advisors while still building teams that one day will take their full-time attention to manage. Best of all, when our agents retire or pass away, they can select a pre-allocated beneficiary who will continue earning income from the business they've developed with us. I remember when we announced to Frank De Lio that he qualified for Platinum Legacy Ownership for the business he has built, he started to cry. It was at that point that it really hit him - that his wife, Yolanda, and their three girls, will never need for money ever again. Frank, and many others, have built businesses that will continue in their family tree for generations to come. This, my friends, is a first of its kind in the IMO/MGA world!

* **You see, in combining both of these models, our agents are able to build enough residual income to retire at the time of their choosing.**

Pension plans, which are going the way of the dinosaur anyway, may pay you up to 60% or 70% of your income when you retire, but it comes at the expense of so much work until you don't have time left to enjoy your retirement. With Experior, agents who build faster are free to retire faster. In fact, there are agents on our team who've only worked with us for five years and are talking about retirement in their early forties.

The beauty of all of this is that we have a commitment to develop and support part-time agents in the same way we would full-time agents. When I started out as a father to two children - which quickly became four - I needed to pay my bills with supplemental income to get by. The industry at the time, however, didn't allow part-time agents in Canada. In many companies, you're strongly discouraged and, in some cases, not even allowed to start part-time. Sadly, most new agents don't realize that they need to have a stockpile of living expenses (generally 6-12 months) to build their businesses.

Experior trains agents 7-15 times a week. We're on Zoom webinars and WhatsApp, Telegram, or Facebook daily. The camaraderie, culture, and celebration in our team culture is second to none. You hear about a lot of Silicon Valley offices with fancy coffee makers, ping pong tables, and other exotic frills to develop camaraderie, but, especially since 2020, a lot of those fabricated, fancy rooms are empty. Real camaraderie comes from celebrating one another, supporting one another, and, above all, every person in the organization being treated as a human being.

A couple of months ago I was at one of our offices in Edmonton, Alberta, when an agent approached me to say, "Jamie, I want to thank you."

"You bet, Melvie," I responded.

"No, really, I'm so happy. I just bought my first home. I'm a single mom and moved here from the Philippines, and I honestly never thought this could happen."

"High five! I'm so proud of you!"

"Yeah, I'm just shy of hitting a hundred thousand in annual income with Experior now... I may even quit my job soon."

My jaw hit the floor when I realized what Melvie was sharing with me.

"Wait, what?! You're part-time? And a single mom?"

That moment was, for Lee-Ann and I, like Christmas wrapped up in a single moment. This is one of the reasons we knew that when creating Experior, we had to provide the same care and attention to our part-time agents as our full-timers. Would any other MGA/IMO or large agency kill for Melvie's talent? Absolutely, but they are generally too short-sighted to see and appreciate it.

Compensation

I would love to detail compensation for you in this book, but as we continue to expand into new U.S. and worldwide territories, the products and licensing vary. Therefore, if you're looking for specific numbers in our compensation plans, head over to:

USA: www.ExperiorUSAVideo.com
Canada: www.ExperiorCanadaVideo.com

Shares in Experior

Whether or not Experior goes public, shares in the company are another valuable bonus we add to compensation once an agent hits the Executive Director level. Executive Directors receive 2,000 company shares. When you become a Senior Executive Director, you receive 3,000 shares. National Executive Directors receive 4,000 shares, and Senior National Executive Directors receive 5,000. Few things bring a brighter smile to my face than hearing Executive Director Raza Begg say, "What CEO gives away 21% in equity shares back to his team, and they aren't stopping? I'll tell you, here in America, there are none." Our agents are building a company within a company, but they also own a piece of the mothership.

Is This Realistic?

In a word: YES. In two words: HELL, YES! You don't need to have a team of 1,000, 500, 200, or even 10 people to achieve these levels. You can become an agency owner with just seven licensed agents.

Agents such as Mauro Arturi and Darren Golka have just crossed over 600 licensed agents in Canada. Frank De Lio has crossed over 500 agents, also in Canada, and we haven't even scratched the surface in the United States yet, where we just recently started building in 2021. Our team of "Crazy Americans" in Maryland - Aurelio Evans, Dr. Meri Robinson, and Erik Robinson

- built an organization of over 70 licensed agents before they were with Experior for a full year. And they have zero experience in the industry to boot.

Raza and Imrana Begg began writing business in June of 2021 and on December 31st, 2021, they became our number one personal producers. Raza and Imrana did $35,000 in personal production in June of 2021, $55,000 in July, $53,000 in August, and the husband and wife team were up to $294,000 in personal production in their first six months. There's a lot of meat on that bone; there's a veritable feast to be had for our future U.S. agents.

Having fun, rapping Vanilla Ice on stage in front of 800 Experior agents at our 2020 convention where Vanilla Ice was a guest speaker

The Experior Difference

Equity Ownership

As mentioned above, our agents enjoy equity ownership in Experior. You can become an owner in the company as soon as you reach the Executive Director level of production. Some men and women have achieved equity ownership within just six months of joining Experior.

Vesting

Our agents are business owners vested from day one in our company. With some companies, you'll wait two years to become vested. Not here. Even more importantly, a lot of the agents who come to us feeling frustrated that their previous MGAs/IMOs hold their business for six months after they leave, some for even up to two years. When an agent leaves Experior, we don't hold anyone for any period of time whatsoever. We release books instantly when an agent leaves Experior, which is in line with the integrity of our business-owner values.

Technology Tools

We currently invest a little over $20,000 a week into our technology tools. Executive Director Mark Ferland was delighted to see that, while watching dozens of agents he knows in other companies suffer during a halt in business during the pandemic, Experior didn't miss a beat because we weren't reliant on outside-rented software. Whilst renting software for commissions, training, CRMs, proposals, learning systems, and other back-office technology would be cheaper, it slows down agencies. We have Lee-Ann to thank for adamantly insisting that we don't rent any software, both for security reasons as well as so that agents would have the ability to custom-build their experience as they grow and as we grow as a company. At first, some of the team were a little irked by the tremendous amount of work and time that this required, but today, our custom technology makes us hands-down one of the greatest insurance agencies in the world, and number one in the world very soon.

Marketing

We don't market Experior, but we market our agents. Our Head Office is staffed with 30 individuals; six of whom are solely invested in marketing our agents. Our agents come up with progressive, avant-garde, and even downright crazy marketing ideas. They run them past the marketing team, and we'll support them to elegantly and tactfully, compliantly marketing in their unique ways. You'll love to read about the various creative ways that Dr. Meri and Erik Robinson have used to generate interest in their U.S. organization in Part Two.

Leads

The bane of so many salespeople's existence. Here in Canada, we've had the luck of not having to generate leads to become a leading insurance agency. We built the company in a warm market, friend-to-friend, neighbor-to-neighbor. However, in the U.S., this is of paramount concern to our new American agents. We've developed a system for these agents to garner leads, costing anywhere from $0.75 up to $42 per lead, including appointment-booking abilities and personal messaging delivered straight to the agent's inbox. Experior doesn't earn a penny on these highly-discounted leads that are generated. I've heard of other IMOs who, in fact, mark up the price of leads so much that it's a substantial revenue generator to their bottom line. They make more money selling leads than they do selling insurance.

Transparency

When we run our payroll every week, our agents get weekly statements that show every single sale that took place, every customer, policy number, every carrier that they sold for, and the amount of premium or commission that they earned on that customer. All of this is also securely stored in our back office. Some of our big leaders get weekly statements that now exceed 400 pages because of the custom-built payroll system we've developed that itemizes every single penny our agents earn. In other organizations, agents may need to run from carrier to carrier to reconcile commissions.

Turnkey System

We currently charge just $150 for somebody to register with Experior, and between $19-$79 monthly in systems fees to run their organization with full transparency, along with tools to quote and help agents develop a professional financial analysis for the everyday consumer. This also includes the ability to run compliant email campaigns, an a CRM system built in, so agents don't have to spend a fortune elsewhere for these valuable tools.

Timing

For our agents in the U.S., as well as Canada, you have an absolute ground-floor opportunity. Periodically, somebody will tell me that they want to represent a company that's been around for 10, 20, or 30 years because it represents stability to that agent. Conceptually, I understand what they're saying. But think about this: most people in the insurance industry are entrepreneurs. They don't want to squeeze blood from a turnip, going up against agents who've invested 30 years building businesses in that organization. In the Practice Company that Frank, Mauro, Laval, and myself came from, we'd have made millions of dollars if we'd started on the ground floor in the seventies and eighties when it was new.

Entrepreneurs want to say, "I help put that company on the map." We're not looking for another salesperson who'll be happy to peddle life insurance for the rest of their lives. Although insurance is a necessary part of our business, there's a point at which you burnout, which is common with the

Personal Producer Model mentioned above.

We're looking for entrepreneurs and builders. After two, three, or four years, you can move from the transactional day-to-day individual client ministry role to a leader. *That's* the Experior difference. We aren't producers. We aren't even solely builders. We're entrepreneurs.

Retention

As illustrated in *the A Word of Warning About Network Marketing and MLM* section above, a lot of Builder Model agencies suffer from poor retention, with 44% of new recruits on average dropping out after just a year with the organization, 90% dropping out within five years, and almost 100% of recruits dropping out by tear ten.

Experior has an 85% retention rate year-on-year. That means that you are not running a revolving door, not just recruiting to replace, but rather recruiting to build. With retention rates this high, our model allows agents to recruit with the peace of mind that 85% of their recruits will stay. In our biggest competitors, retention rates are still only 60-65%. This forces the agent to continually recruit without growing their organization quickly and efficiently.

Legacy Ownership

Later in this book, you'll hear the stories of Andrea Rogers and Tzachi Chen, two of our Executive Directors who went to bat for this Legacy Ownership Model. Essentially this means that when an agent dies, their business can be inherited by a beneficiary. In other organizations, your business dies with you. With Experior, your family will receive 75% of the commissions on your code or book of business as soon as you hit Executive Director level. Agents such as Ryan Tongs joined Experior for this very reason, and it attracts excellent agents almost daily who are free to bring this contractual agreement to their lawyer or accountant to make it a part of their estate planning. We've even recently rolled out Gold, Platinum, and Platinum Plus Legacy Ownership, where your heirs or your estate can get paid indefinitely on the business you build with Experior.

Executive Director Raza Begg learned about Experior from his friend Jacques Vaughan, along with his wife Merideth, who are now also Executive Directors with Experior themselves in Maryland, U.S.A. I must add, it took him seven attempts to pass his exams, but he didn't quit! What a stud! Now he and his wife too are growing an amazing organization.

Raza and Imrana Begg

Begg told me, "You had me at the legacy ownership" when he initially began researching Experior Financial Group. You see, Raza looks to be the epitome of good health. He is a former professional ballroom dancer who trained NFL Football Player Emmitt Smith to win *Dancing With The Stars* in 2006. However, he soon thereafter underwent a quadruple bypass and nearly died on the operating table. He was given a second chance, but he is uninsurable. This is an unfathomable burden for a father of four children, currently aged 25, 14, 11, and 5. One afternoon, Jacques called Raza and said, "Hey, I'm thinking of joining this new insurance agency, Experior Financial Group. Will you check it out and give me your opinion?" Both Raza and his wife Imrana Begg joined Experior almost immediately thereafter, getting licensed in May 2021. For Raza, Legacy Ownership means that the business he builds with Experior Financial Group is his life insurance plan. With this assurance in mind (and in contract), he put the pedal to the metal in mid-2021 and is now our number one personal producer, beating all other agents in the U.S. and Canada. He calls it "generational residual income" and "the ultimate peace of mind."

Do you want to see your beneficiary inherit your business before you pass? The Legacy Ownership is also a buyout that allows you to live your legacy while you're still living. Do you own what you're building? Do you feel like the king or queen that you are? Does your family feel secure that you're providing for them? Are you stuck living paycheck to paycheck, trading hours for dollars? Or are you an entrepreneur?

In Part Two of this book, we'll dive into stories from over 20 different agents in Experior, from all walks of life, to illustrate to you the keys to building a great business. Whether you're in insurance sales, real estate, retail, consulting, or any other business under the sun: this next part is for you.

Chapter Five Lessons:

#1: Success is an equal opportunity employer. Your opportunity awaits, you just have to decide.

#2: You've heard it said that the best money is made when you're solving a problem. Lee-Ann and I saw that there was a problem with the traditional IMO/MGA Models. We also saw the value in the Builders and Captive Models in various agencies in our industry, so we captured lightning in a bottle and combined the three of them for an insurance agency like nothing that's ever been seen. How can you eliminate the negative aspects of your industry by shaking things up and building a system that takes what's working in a progressive, innovative way? How can you, like me and Lee-Ann, align with partners who can pull it off? We're nothing without a team!

Part Two

Keys To Great Leadership

Chapter Six

Great Leaders Are Critical to Building A Great Company

"To build a long-term, successful enterprise, when you don't close a sale, open a relationship."
Patricia Fripp

"I think the most important thing about coaching is that you have to have a sense of confidence about what you're doing. You have to be a salesman, and you have to get your players, particularly your leaders, to believe in what you're trying to accomplish on the basketball floor."
Phil Jackson

People regularly interview me and ask, "Jamie, how did you and Lee-Ann grow the company so fast? How do you recruit so many people?" It's not hard for me to answer this question: "We have great leaders in our business." It keeps me humble to shine the light on our agents and the leaders within Experior. But also, it's true.

When a team is run by a good leader, that team can win. Just look at NBA Hall of Fame Coach Phil Jackson. Jackson took the Chicago Bulls from nothing to a dynasty in the nineties, winning six NBA Championships. Could lightning strike twice? Was Jackson's success due to the incredible players on his team, including Scottie Pippen, Michael Jordan, and more?

When Jordan retired, Jackson joined the Los Angeles Lakers shortly after. That team was struggling, but Jackson led them summarily to five NBA Championships.

The numbers don't lie:

Chicago Bulls NBA Championships: 1991, 1992, 1993, 1996, 1997, 1998
Los Angeles Lakers NBA Championships: 2000, 2001, 2002, 2009, 2010

Some argue that these eleven NBA Championships didn't have anything to do with Jackson but are a reflection of having great players on his teams. Yes and no. Why did Jackson have the best players on his team? Because he was the best coach. Jackson raised everyone's game to levels they couldn't achieve without him.

The success of the Bulls, between 1991 and 1998, and the Lakers, between 2000 and 2010, was due to a combination of an excellent leader and excellent followers. The players from those respective teams relay stories from that era, speaking about their time with those Championship teams as though it was something mystical, like something out of a dream.

For the Bulls, that era came to an end when ego crept in; Jerry Krause, who was the general manager at that time, wasn't feeling the love. He was unhappy with the credit Jackson had been receiving about the Bulls' Championships and felt underappreciated. Some reports even hinted that Krause believed Jackson was indebted to him for giving him his first coaching job. Rather than celebrate the success of Phil Jackson, he wanted to have more focus on himself.

For the Lakers, it was well known that Shaquille O'Neal and Kobe Bryant did not want to play together. They were both superstars, and neither wanted to take a back seat to the other. When there are issues at the top, all players on the team are affected; it dampens spirits, destroys camaraderie, and eventually, it can hit your bank account.

When it comes to success as a leader, if the team is winning, it's because of the team. If the team is losing, it's because of you. This is a hard pill to swallow, but I have learned that you elevate others, by elevating others.

I want to see your organization run with this level of leadership and, in this second part of our story, I'll detail a few more stories to illustrate how Experior has mastered the art of leadership that inspires, motivates, and elevates our agents.

Great Leadership Lessons:

#1: A great leader raises everyone's game to levels they couldn't achieve without him or her.

#2: A great leader is nothing without a great team.

Chapter Seven

Great Leaders Use Motivation Vs. Manipulation

"The difference between the impossible and the possible lies in a man's determination."
Tommy Lasorda

"Blood, sweat, and respect.
The first two you give.
The last you earn.
Give it. Earn it."
The Rock

Let's pretend that I'm going to train you to make a fortune in real estate. Come to my seminar (for which I'll charge you $4,000 to attend) and I'll walk you through, step-by-step, how to buy and sell real estate. With as little as zero dollars down and paying me $4,000 to attend, I will make you rich.

While you attend my seminar, I will regurgitate things I've read over the years, including the same CD/tape cassettes every other business professional has listened to from the eighties and nineties about being a winner and achieving success. The one caveat is this: I have never sold or bought a piece of real estate in my life. But damn can I preach a great message about changing your life and winning!

Let's say I have a killer website. I take professional photos regularly with fake backdrops on private jets, driving luxury vehicles, or at the beach. I create nonstop content which would cause the discerning eye to wonder when it is that I actually work, as opposed to talking about working. I'll tell you how to live the life I've achieved in my $25,000 weekend retreat. You can be an exceptional business coach, just like me. The problem is that I've never actually generated value in a business. I teach others how to teach others to become business coaches. Nobody runs a business, we just all give people the opportunity to take tens of thousands of dollars from others in a never-ending loop of coaches coaching others to become coaches, with nobody having run an actual business or created any real value in the world.

Pyramid schemes. Manipulation. Anybody with a few slides and a screen can plagiarize something they read in a book and motivate people temporarily. That's called manipulation. But to truly motivate people, charisma and charm will only get you so far. People will come up against hardships and you won't know how to help them through those challenges. You'll be exposed as the fraud you are.

Some great leaders are charismatic, confident, polished, and excellent on stage or in front of an audience. But in Experior, we've found that the most truly successful leaders understand motivation. Any business owner or leader wants a motivated team. However, when poor leaders don't know how to motivate, they manipulate instead. Managers say, "do this." Leaders say, "let's go."

Branding shares a fine line with motivation. Regularly, new agents will approach me and ask, "Jamie, do you have any tips on branding?" I hesitate because I don't know if they're looking for help creating TikTok content or color schemes on Instagram, both of which I see almost no value in doing.

I tell them this: your reputation precedes you, but your character precedes your reputation. Remember: your character will eventually be exposed. Your brand is who you are, and everything you do. How you do one thing is how you do anything; you can't fool people for long with a snazzy image when your heart isn't there. So, focus on blessing people, and you will find that prospecting will become a thing of the past.

Madhab Dulal is a great example of this. I asked him how he has built a quarter of a million in income with our business in just two years. He explained to me how he became the magnet. He began consulting with a charity where people were struggling to pay the final expenses when somebody passed.

"Helping people in their time of need generated so much goodwill that my business began to sail. I didn't have to pick up the phone, I just began helping people."

In his unmistakable, timeless southern Georgia drawl, Art Williams would say to a crowd of 50,000 people, "Nobody will believe in, or follow, a negative, dull, disillusioned, frustrated, dadgum, crybaby! People want leaders who are positive, excited, enthusiastic, and tough!"

When you have true passion for what you're selling, there is no need to manipulate people. Nothing draws people to you more than enthusiasm. Nothing helps your team feel truly inspired by the work they're doing than to see your own genuine enthusiasm for your clients and your products. Motivation is what makes us leaders, manipulation makes us dictators.

Motivator or Manipulator?

Manipulator	Motivator
Cares only about the work being done by a person.	Cares about the PERSON.
It's all about the show. Words.	Substance is non-negotiable. Actions.
Empty promises, false hopes, broken dreams.	Purposeful leadership, bank account reflects your hard work.

Mauro Arturi is patient, curiously quiet, and an exceptional listener, but his composure has a shadow side: Mauro can get mad. The Experior "Godfather" as we call him, is one of the most relationship-driven and loving leaders I've ever met; I remember the first time Daniel Prete shared with me that he couldn't leave Mauro, even when he lost everything at their previous company. He knew that Mauro would make it right; he trusted his leader.

Mauro has a breaking point that is the result of a combination of having watched his team struggle and experiencing his own lack of success. He shares an unforgettable story with his agency that illustrates several critical things about motivation versus manipulation

One fateful afternoon Mauro drove through blinding rain to a Senior National Sales Director meeting in Toronto with his former company. The entire meeting already felt like a big joke.

You see, at the time, despite being paraded for his leadership, Mauro wasn't having great success with the company to which he'd end up devoting 19 years to and leaving as a Vice President.

Like so many men and women who were recognized as "high achievers" in that company, the majority of them were struggling. A title meant to imply success to their peers and their agents, but countless "Vice Presidents" and "Leaders" could barely afford gas in their cars. I was one of them and, for a period, so was Mauro.

There was no driving without wipers that afternoon; the rain was completely blinding, hitting the windshield with such a smack that you'd have to yell at the passenger sitting seven inches away to be heard. And those damn wipers wouldn't budge. Now, at this company, you'd be made to feel bad if you went to a funeral over a sales meeting. So, Mauro dug around the pockets in his back seat to find some twine, which I imagine he and his wife Mara were going to use for an epic bresaola later that night, but I'm not shy about Italian stereotypes. Maybe the twine was there to use as backup shoelaces, I don't know.

But on this particular afternoon, Mauro tied the twine to his windshield wiper. For the entire trip across the city, Mauro yanked that twine back and forth while he drove.

When he left the Practice Company, Mauro was at just about 100% of his income capacity, in the top 1% of income earners there. He had 40 agents in his organization. Today, Mauro has over 650 licensed agents on his team. He left one of his best friends of 37 years when he came to Experior and this man, who'd been manipulated and brow-beaten by the previous company, chose to forfeit his relationship with Mauro. Almost as if Mauro was leaving a cult, he became an enemy overnight by simply making a decision that would ultimately prove to be better for him, his family, his team, and his clients.

Now one thing about Mauro that everybody knows him for is that he's a relationships guy. He loves his team and was even the best man at one of his agent's weddings. When he came to me and told me he needed to attract this friend over to Experior, I didn't try to sell the guy on our potential. I didn't tell him I'd give him special incentives or titles either. I didn't try to manipulate him. I sought, rather, to use this challenge as a chance to improve the comp plan for our entire company to win this guy over.

He didn't come. People are afraid of prosperity. In a way, it's like an abused spouse who knows intellectually that they deserve better but doesn't *feel* worthy. When people don't feel worthy, when they choose to suffer, when they can't leave abuse because of the fancy titles and cult-like ganging up on the competition without provocation; that's manipulation, not motivation.

In the financial services industry, manipulation is endemic, which is why our Chief Experience Officer Shelden Smollan, a guy who got started in the industry before I was born, says, "Experior marks the end of the MGA system as we know it."

As I see it, everybody in our company is a leader. Either you're like Mauro Arturi and Andrea Rogers, who essentially coach their teams all day, or you're the newest agent on the block educating a client about various life insurance products or investment solutions; we're all leaders. And if you're reading this book, you're either a leader or you want to become one.

But what kind of leader do you want to be? Do you motivate or manipulate?

Both mine and Lee-Ann's hearts break when we hear stories of people being manipulated into loyalty with their companies. I'm floored at the tricks and games that have been played. When Dror David began prospecting experienced agents with another company, there were entire Facebook groups and forums devoted to chastising him, calling him "evil" for prospecting agents with that firm and that they should never join Experior. Well, despite this ridicule, he has become one of the most successful agents in our company, yet he joined us with zero experience in sales or the financial industry, plus he's just 33 years old. He didn't bring a team of agents with him or have hundreds of clients. He worked like a dog and climbed the ranks.

In Chapter One you saw me discuss the tortoise and the hare. In the fable, the tortoise wins because he's consistent. Consistency bears immeasurable compound interest. Consistency trumps natural gifts every time. But what if we put a third species in that race? A dog. This is the *next level.*

When my dogs are off-leash in my back yard they'll run for hours, and it's nearly impossible to get them to settle down. When there's room to run; they don't stop. When we give our dogs space, freedom, and trust; they are as happy as an animal could be. Their energy is truly remarkable. They're totally in the zone.

But what makes those dogs happy is knowing that they're free but also still being led. When I, their leader, gets in the car and makes like I'm going to leave, they'll be at my side faster than I can say, "here, girl!"

My agents are free to run, but I'm there as their leader. Not their boss, but their coach. The more successful they are, the more successful I am. They're not pawns. They're my family. I love to watch them thrive and have fun in business while earning hundreds of thousands of dollars a year.

About one year after Mauro joined us in business, he and I were sitting down in his office while his team was running a career seminar. I'm babbling on about some compensation plan or contract when Mauro sets his phone down in front of me. It was a text from his wife, Mara, with a photo of her and his two boys holding a bunch of bags after some back-to-school shopping.

The text simply read "Thank you so much for making a change."

That image of Mauro's happy family is forever burned in my head. I looked up at Mauro.

"Thank you, sir, this is why we do what we do."

Great Leadership Lessons:

#1: A great leader will motivate, not manipulate.

#2: Your reputation precedes you, but your character precedes your reputation. Remember: your character will eventually get exposed. Your brand is who you are, and everything you do. How you do one thing is how you do anything; you can't fool people long with a snazzy image when your heart isn't there. So focus on blessing people, and you will find that prospecting will become a thing of the past.

#3: Managers say, "do this." Leaders say, "let's go."

Chapter Eight

Great Leaders Value Mindset Over Skillset

"Determination is the strength needed to succeed."
Dan Gable

"You're never a loser until you quit trying."
Mike Ditka

A few months ago, one of our Executive Directors, Frank De Lio, called me and said, "I've got an idea for training and supporting my team, and I want your input." De Lio shared a story I'll never forget.

He went on to explain that 20 years ago, his friend and business partner Mauro won a trip to Miami Beach, Florida, with a company they'd been working with. Mauro had recruited Frank and wanted him to be inspired by the trip, sharing in the reward Mauro had received as an esteemed Top Producer in the company. Funnily enough, although being esteemed and regarded as Top Producer, Mauro didn't have money to put gas in his car at the time, and Frank didn't have it either.

While preparing for the trip, Frank shared with his mother that he was proud to be going on the trip where his business idol would take the stage that weekend. Frank's mom knew how hard the financial services industry was and handed him two hundred bucks in cash for "incidentals."

"Ma, I don't need this, I'm a businessman."

"Just take it, honey. You never know when there'll be emergencies while you're traveling."

What Mrs. De Lio didn't know was that both Mauro and Frank were broke, having all of $20 between them to survive for the week. If it weren't for Frank's mom, the two would have starved during that conference.

Frank and Mauro sat at a table one night during the pinnacle moment of the event, stuffing bread rolls in their suit jacket pockets when suddenly, Frank felt a hand gently on his shoulder. The entire room began buzzing around him; excited whispers peppered the atmosphere. When Frank looked up, he saw "The Man", Hector, squeezing past him, cutting through tables in the crowded banquet room towards the stage. Hector was Frank's idol, and he still has the utmost respect for him.

It was no sooner than Mauro said, "Man, you better never wash that jacket," that the room erupted in deafening applause; it was like Bon Jovi had just taken the stage. At that moment, Frank shared with me that he knew he wanted to have that effect on people too. Hector was a Top Earner in the company where Mauro and De Lio were floundering, despite having earned accolades as "Top Producers." He was pulling about $3 million a year at that time, but instead of hoarding the secrets for himself, he led weekly training sessions that were available to anybody in the world, and to my knowledge, still are.

Frank's parents got ripped off by an insurance agent decades ago. His dad was uninsurable due to health reasons, but some slimeball agent had the De Lios' four children insured excessively, saying, "If something happens to Mr. De Lio, you'll receive $50,000 from each of your kids' policies, Mrs. De Lio."

Several years later Mauro Arturi, a family friend who'd grown up near Frank's dad in Italy, came by the house. Mrs. De Lio handed the policies to Mauro, whose face immediately sunk. He looked at all four policies on Frank and his siblings several times, looking for something that wasn't there.

"This can't be," he muttered. Mrs. De Lio's face dropped too when Mauro finally uttered, "Mrs. De Lio, you're completely vulnerable. Mr. De Lio isn't insured." When Frank's father called the agent's office, he found out that the weasel had vanished from the industry and later had been charged with defrauding other families like the De Lios. It was at that moment that Frank knew he'd join the industry where he could right those wrongs; he'd turn the pain on his mother's face into joy for other families.

Frank didn't succeed in the industry until well after his first decade, and after 15 years he only had 20 agents under him and was making $160,000 annually. I'll never forget one night, when we were locking up the office in the early days of Experior, when he placed his hand on my shoulder and said, "Jamie, I'm gonna work as if I own this company."

You better damn well believe he did. Just two years into his work with Experior, Frank had over 100 people in his organization, with some earning over $100,000 annually in their first and second years with Experior, where they used to earn just $20,000 annually with their former company.

"So, here's the plan, Jamie. I'm going to run a weekly training session called Mindset Over Skillset. I want people to know that winning is a mental game. They don't have to be smart or independently wealthy to make it here at Experior, they just have to believe." This was one of those moments that I wanted to drive to Toronto and hug Frank, but since he's a pretty tough guy, I held myself back.

"Frank, you couldn't be more accurate. What can I do to support you?"

Today, Frank runs an organization with over 550 licensed agents at Experior. He's cleaning over $500,000 of passive annual income (and it continues to rise every month) and has made countless men and women financially free, both as clients and as agents on his team because he gets it. Almost every month he is popping out new six-figure income earners. He's the Experior Spirit. It's mindset over skillset.

I remember one time in late 2016, after the FML team of Frank De Lio, Mauro Arturi, and Laval Dubeau joined us, things got heated in the attorney's office where we were defending ourselves against accusations from my former company. I felt like we were innocent of any of their accusations, but people didn't want me to keep fighting. I didn't know what to do when the attorneys walked out of the room to confer with the opposing counsel. The tension was killing me - I literally couldn't sit still. I saw an opportunity to remove some of the stress in the form of an empty 18 or so inches on the wall in the conference room where there wasn't an overpriced, bad print of a bridge or a peaceful river, and, before I knew it, I was upside down in a handstand against the wall. Frank looked concerned and broke the silence in the best way possible.

"Well, Prickett. We're here because you're borderline genius, and borderline crazy. You're illustrating that point perfectly right here and now."

Periodically, I read business articles and magazines where editors suggest that so many jobs will become redundant once robots and AI replace them. I've wondered about the time when I have a legal issue and instead of paying a $15,000 retainer to some law office, I'll be guided through a script on an app and the AI will show me exactly what forms I need to file. The app may even pre-fill most of my information and tell me where I need to send the forms. Perhaps I'll use an e-signature and file them directly from my phone, in the car perhaps, while I'm on my way to the office.

But do you know one thing AI will never replace? Leadership. Management, however, it may. Managers focus on keeping people on assembly lines; producing without thinking outside the box, lest we slow down the line. Managers control efficiencies; they tell people what to do, how to do it, and where to do it. As for me, I'm a terrible manager. I've done it well, but it's not my happy place by any means.

Similarly, I don't like to train managers, either. I want to see Frank thinking outside the box; giving his team mindset skills that will help them become greater leaders. Baljit Parmar, an Executive Director living in Alberta, Canada, is a great leader with us. I recently spent time hosting an event for other leaders at Baljit's home. His wife loves to cook homemade Indian food when they entertain and Baljit loves the bar and gaming room downstairs in his new home which is, coincidentally, breathtaking. I said to him, "Baljit, what is your goal for your agents this year?"

He recalled a story he'd read recently; the man reads voraciously to improve his craft as a leader and financial representative. In the story, he'd read about a time Victor Frankl said, "Do you know the problem with America? We have a Statue of Liberty, but not a Statue of Responsibility."

"I want more of our leaders to not merely strategize in our organization's mastermind, but I want more of them to courageously review mistakes they make so that we can improve together."

"And what about you, Baljit? What mistakes do you regret?"

"I don't have many regrets, but I once worked with a man named Curtis in construction. At the time, Curtis wasn't making that much more than me, not enough to make him a millionaire... or so I thought. After working as a fry cook, a taxi driver, and even a dishwasher when I came to Canada, somebody told me that I could make ten times the income in construction. What I gained didn't come from an increase in salary, but from the relationships I began to build with influential, intelligent investors such as Curtis.

Baljit Parmar

"One day, my friend invited me to his cottage. Now, in India, a cottage means four walls and a sparsely decorated thousand square foot room. Not Curtis's cottage: it was a mansion on the lake with at least five, maybe six thousand square feet. I said to myself, 'Curtis is one of my dearest friends. But he's living a life of luxury. What do I need to do differently?'

"I didn't play the victim and blame my skin color. I didn't blame my accent or my status as an immigrant. Rather, I took responsibility for my own education and mindset. I began reading Napoleon Hill, Jim Rohn, and I've committed Steve Siebold's *177 Mental Toughness Secrets of the World Class* to memory; even traveling to Atlanta, Georgia to meet the author.

"Since starting with Experior in March of 2018, I've seen people in my team, such as Raju Brar, go from never having made more than $30,000 a year to making over $100,000 for three consecutive years. Prakash Bashyal hit $100,000, and he's the recruit of one of my mentees and fellow Mastermind participant Madhab Dulal, who's hit over a quarter of a million annually. My team earned over $2.5 million in commissions in 2021. My only known regret is that I didn't start 10 or 15 years ago. But even in that, I take responsibility. Now that I have the mindset, the mental toughness, there is no end to the success my team and I will have. Because Experior is a ground floor company, I even have time to catch up to my friends who began wisely investing decades before me."

Great Leadership Lessons:

#1: You absolutely have the skills to succeed. Mindset trumps skillset, every time. The Experior Spirit is Mindset over Skillset.

#2: Great leaders review mistakes and keep evolving.

Chapter Nine

Great Leaders Make Promises They Can Keep

"If it weren't for the dark days, we wouldn't know what it is to walk in the light."
Earl Campbell

I love telling people the story of Lee-Ann and me breaking down on our way to a conference with our practice company where we were being celebrated as leaders in the industry. I don't feel ashamed that I devoted ten years to a company where we were living paycheck to paycheck. I'm not embarrassed that we invested almost two years building Empirical Group only to have it stolen out from us. I'm not even ashamed that our Practice Company dragged Team FML, Lee-Ann, and myself through a brutal six-month lawsuit that cost the five of us entrepreneurs in the startup phase of our business nearly $400,000 for crimes we didn't commit.

I am fueled by the broken promises in our industry. I recently spent time with Experior Executive Director Daniel Prete, who told me that he could retire in three or four years because of the passive income he is building with his business at Experior. In Daniel's previous business he made a maximum of $6,000 in his best year. This is absolutely bewildering considering he was there for eight years.

Daniel & Ashley Prete

Maybe he had a crappy leader or upline? Nope. His upline was Mauro Arturi, the man who was also the best man at Prete's wedding a few years ago. Mauro's current team of 650 licensed agents earns an average of $54,000 annually, and countless agents on that team work part-time. Was Daniel a total moron? Wrong again. He's making a quarter of a million dollars annually with Experior and made $100,000 in his second year. He's intelligent, heart-centered, and very strategic about what he does.

The difference is that Mauro and Prete's previous company continually dangled a carrot in front of them. This is an epidemic both among other "Builder Models" or MLM companies as well as the insurance industry as a whole. Just one big recruit can make your whole year; just one big investment client. There's always hope... but until Prete joined Experior, that was false hope. Great leaders make promises they can keep. Manipulators dangle carrots. The carrot-dangling promise-breakers may recruit hundreds or even thousands of agents with false hopes, but lasting leaders and successful companies keep their promises. They may not recruit as many people as the razzle-dazzle pyramid scheme salesmen, but they'll keep the people they recruit happy over a longer period of time. What's more, they'll hang their hats on a better reputation, which we'll discuss further in Chapter Seventeen.

Matthew Stewart giving back to the community at the Edmonton Food Bank

Experior Executive Director Matthew Stewart had a similar experience with broken promises. He labored for six years under the impression that he owned his book of business with his former company, the same one from which Darren Golka, Andrea Rogers, and so many other successful agents in our organization came from. Stewart was called a "Senior Marketing Director" at his previous company; they called him "top tier" in the industry, but after his father got sick and he chose to move across the country to be with his family, Stewart was told he couldn't keep his team. After six years in the industry, he was destitute. He tells me now, "you know, Jamie. It was right there in my contract. It couldn't have been clearer. Everything I'd built belonged to somebody else."

It took just two years with Experior for Matthew to hit the $100,000 mark in revenue - a threshold he hadn't reached previously in his total of 12 years in the industry. If Matthew decides to make another change, we release his code and allow him to take his business with him on Day One. I don't think he's going anywhere, though.

Adding insult to injury is the nasty game of bad-mouthing that is rampant in the financial industry. Francis Sinday and his wife, Dianne, built a business called Stellar Wealth Solutions from 2015, operating through to 2017. The Sindays struggled in this country for over ten years, floundering in finance, hitting success, only to have it stolen from them not once, but twice. I resonate with his story because it resembles mine and Lee-Ann's; the Sindays were misled by broken promises.

You see, the Sindays' former company, where they worked before they started Stellar Wealth Solutions, is a blister on the Canadian Insurance scene with their misleading marketing and cookie-cutter insurance solutions that don't work for the many families they foil. That dishonest company sued Francis and Dianne, threatened by how quickly the Sindays had built a successful team with their new venture. They were bombarded with criticism and false information, some even coming from their own recruits who abandoned them during this time.

Francis and Dianne Sinday

At the end of 2017, Lee-Ann and I performed a sneak attack on Francis and his wife in a hotel where we were staying on a business trip out to Calgary, Alberta. One night, a friend told them to meet somebody in the lobby of the hotel. Dianne and Francis thought they'd be recruiting somebody to their agency. Instead, Lee-Ann and I sat with them until past midnight and told our story, assuring them that nobody could ever "fire" them from their own business when Experior was behind them. They joined us in 2018 and, within a year, became the number one agency in Experior. Prior to getting on their feet, Dianne and Francis considered sending their children back "home" to the Philippines to live with family while they got back on their feet. Also being a father of four at the time (they now have a fifth), the thought always made me sick to my stomach. The abuse that Dianne and Francis endured is another reason I have the fire in my belly to get out there and help our agents become successful every day.

When you see the broken promises and abuse our agents have sustained from other companies, it's hard not to get discouraged by the amount of pure evil there is out there. It can make a strong man weep to see how others are abused across the financial industry. A particularly morbid unsubstantiated promise that I often see other companies make is that "you're joining a team so close, we're like family."

Well, I don't know about you, but in my family, come hell or high water; you have a home in my home. As a leader of leaders, I keep my promises. I don't love people based on performance; a great leader is fair. A great leader has integrity. A great leader keeps their promises even when they're being abandoned. Like the Bible story of the prodigal son, Lee-Ann and I have been challenged when our agents leave us. Just as in that story, we release that agent with their inheritance - with the book of business they've built with us. It hurts to see people leave; and we worry that they won't succeed in other businesses, industries, MGAs, IMOs, or models; but it would hurt worse to let that human go off with nothing. They will leave with what we've promised them, and we'll summarily pray for their best. It's not just our promise; it's our contractual obligation to our agents. The flip side of this is that because we treat people fairly, perhaps people who left us believing the grass was greener on the other side, we have had many of them come back to join us again. One example of this is Mario Francella, who you will hear about shortly. He holds a record with Experior for joining us the most. Three times! But you'll soon hear how things are going for him now.

It's common that new recruits in financial services, especially other companies with a Builder's Model, are shown the glossy brochure of how happy and supported they'll be once they join a team. This is common across all industries. Go to any large corporation's "Join Our Team" page on their website and you'll see those promises in big, bold, cheesy stock photos. But all too often, you're left devastated by these false promises.

In 2014, Ryan Tongs' wife was diagnosed with breast cancer. Fortunately, she overcame her illness, but while digging into his own financial security with his former company, he learned that his business would only pay his wife $800 a month if something happened to him. He describes feeling totally naked; like his family had absolutely no security. At that moment, Tongs felt like the Emperor with No Clothes.

This is one of the most fatal flaws people experience in the financial industry; when they die, their business dies with them. You can't designate an heir to take over your business, like having your son or daughter come in and run your restaurant or your gym. You're touted as an "entrepreneur" because you're responsible for building your client base or your downline, but in truth, somebody else has control over your business.

Ryan and Corrine Tongs

Even before the 18 years that Tongs spent with a competitor of ours, Ryan recalls being laid off by another company in a completely separate industry. They thought he was irrelevant; he wasn't earning his keep. After 12 years with that company, he received just a day of severance. The CEO got laid off simultaneously and received a million-dollar bonus. I'll tell you this: Ryan Tongs is anything but irrelevant. He's one of the top producers in our business. After 30 years working for companies that lacked security, Ryan and his wife Corrine are finally appreciated for the value they bring; and paid for it.

Although we're going to spend some time in Part Three talking about immigrants and *Creating A Great Team with Equal Opportunities for Immigrants,* I would be remiss at this point not to honor Susan Caceres and the promise Lee-Ann and I are honored and excited to keep with her.

On December 19th, 2016, Susan moved from Honduras to the U.S. under political asylum. She worked in retail for a natural medicines retailer before becoming licensed in March 2019 with another financial group. In April 2021, she joined Experior and quickly began building her organization, already having promoted two Executive Directors in her first eight months with us.

Lee-Ann and I have particularly loved watching the freedom that this single mom leveraging both the Builder and Personal Producer Models has, who is a full-time parent with a three-year-old daughter who has tragically been born with a disease that leaves her needing even more care than your average time-intensive and totally dependent three-year-old. If you've tried to take your eyes off a three-year-old for 60 seconds, you can visualize the hurdle that any single parent of an otherwise healthy toddler would have working from home while caretaking a child out of school, much less Camila, Susan's adorable daughter.

"How do you do it?" I asked Susan one day while celebrating her enormous accomplishment of 35 licensed team members in just eight months. Susan had achieved as much production in the past 90 days as she'd have done in a year with her previous company.

Susan laughed and admitted, "When I'm on calls, I tell Camila that if she doesn't make any noise, I'll get her a gift!"

I remarked once, "Your daughter has the cutest little freckles, Susan!"

"Camila has melanosis; it's a condition that only affects one out of every half a million children. It gives Camila these black and brown spots that look cute, but it also causes chronic infections."

The challenges don't stop there for this remarkable single parent and exceptionally successful agent. You see, just a few weeks ago, Susan called me to let me know that if she doesn't get a court date scheduled for her visa, she'll lose her political asylum and have to return to Honduras, even though her daughter was born in the U.S. She sounded worried on the phone.

"Jamie, will I lose everything I've built with Experior?"

"Susan, we'll pay you for the rest of your life for the business you have built, even if you get deported. You have my word." Oh, and it's contractual.

If Susan returns to Honduras, although she won't be able to write business, she can leverage the Builder Model to continue building her organization. She'll still get overrides from the work she has done and will continue to do.

Finally, after all the years of living with the threat of their companies not keeping their promises, Daniel Prete, Matthew Stewart, the Sinday family, Ryan Tongs and Susan Caceres are living and prospering in the security of leadership that sets the bar high and keeps their promises.

Great Leadership Lessons:

#1: If you can't take your employer's contract to your accountant or attorney to substantiate the claims they make when they recruit you, you may be vulnerable to having everything you built taken from you in an instant.

#2: Remember: even if you spend 30 years floundering, there is a company or agency out there that will reward you for your brilliance and hard work. It took Ryan Tongs just two years to become a top producer with his new home. Don't. Give. Up.

Chapter Ten

Great Leaders Keep Evolving

"You can raise the bar, or you can wait for others to raise it, but it's getting raised regardless."
Seth Godin

Darren and Stephanie Golka will tell you that when they joined Experior in 2018, I was a bit of a loose cannon. I remember sitting down with Golka one day and getting into a passionate conversation, which is standard. I got heated when the conversation turned towards another industry leader who had publicly bad-mouthed Experior. Although I talk about haters being fuel, it's taken years for me to transmute the knee-jerk reaction of slandering my haters to mindfully thanking them for being so obviously jealous of what and who I am, of being threatened by what Experior is building.

"Prickett, I love you man, but you're off the wall sometimes. Exercise deep breaths and don't respond until you've slept on it. When you're upset or angry, don't speak a word or react in that instant. Respond the next day. Nine times out of ten, what you say the following day will be very different than in the heat of the moment."

Leaders don't just evolve, but they recognize the people who've helped them evolve along the way. I recently texted Golka to thank him for helping me evolve into a better friend, husband, and leader.

Darren & Stephanie Golka

I often refer to “followship before leadership” on Experior team meetings. Followship means being coachable, even though most of the time you may not want to be coached. Followship means going out of your way to learn from the person you are following.

I've never been a huge social media user, but I'm floored at what leaders like Raza and Imrana Begg have taught me about leveraging the platforms they use to keep their teams engaged and the warm referrals coming in. It's been an honor to incorporate Dr. Meri and Erik Robinson's 1-2-3 Sales System into our company training. Few things light Lee-Ann and me up more than seeing our leaders come up with creative ways to market their organizations that aren't in the traditional scope of what has helped us grow our own businesses. Because we are committed to evolution and understanding of what our team needs, they help us grow the entire Experior agency as a whole.

While editing this book I toiled about adding quotes from one of my favorite speakers and a veritable giant in the insurance world. After much consideration, I decided to remove his quotes from the book, even though they're extraordinary and compelling. What's more, I genuinely believe that this man wants what's best for the world and the hundreds of thousands of clients his company has served, but the truth is that this great teacher, now at least 80 years old, hasn't been directly involved with that company for a few decades. His methodologies have become dated, and the result is that the company's clients are no longer provided with the best products that are out there. In turn, the clients aren't as protected as they could be. The agents aren't able to grow wealth as powerfully as they once could, and that breaks my heart. In addition, this once unanimously revered legend in the insurance world founded a company where, today, agents are operating in an antiquated state of mind; and they've become downright predatory. Many of them became stone-cold wealthy and are great people, but they are so far removed from what struggles and issues the people "on the bottom" experience every day. These agents certainly don't benefit from the power that comes from a great reputation, which you'll learn about in Chapter Seventeen.

This leader started a great company, but that company chose not to evolve with the times. Although they were avant-garde, cutting edge, and doing amazing work for their clients and agents in their early years - or at least as good as anything available back then - so many decades later the company has failed to invite more products, carriers, selling systems, and fair compensation for new agents, into their organization.

Nonetheless, I have great respect for this individual and many other pioneers of this great industry, but when you rip the heart out of a booming organization (get rid of the founder that built it), that organization will never be the same. As long as I am healthy and able, I plan to help steer this ship until my last breath. Besides, when do you ever get tired of showing and helping people do more, be more, and have more with their lives?

Some days I spend hours not only listening to the great leaders in my own company but to countless teachers in our industry and others. I'm familiar with all the great sales leaders, business coaches, real estate gurus, and personal development experts. I won't just listen for the feel-good aspect of listening to a great leader. I listen with an open heart and mind: I'm eager to change. I'm eager to evolve. Lee-Ann is no different. This lady learns something new literally every day and continues to grow over the years. Her growth encourages me to keep growing, and vice versa.

Remember: not only is a great leader committed to growth, but a great leader is also a great follower.

Great Leadership Lesson:

A great leader is also a great follower.

Chapter Eleven

Great Leaders Listen

"We have two ears and one mouth, so we should listen more than we say."
Zeno of Citium, as quoted by Diogenes Laërtius

"Every great leader was once a great follower, and the smart ones learn as much from their followers as their followers learn from them."
Jamie Prickett

When Dr. Meri and Erik Robinson, Aurelio Evans, Lee-Ann, and myself sat down one fateful Friday morning in January 2021, Aurelio asked me a bold question.

"Jamie, if we join Experior, how quickly will you open up Maryland?" In early 2021, Experior still hadn't gotten licensed in most of the states; in fact, we were only operating in a select few at that time.

"Aurelio, if you can bring in ten agents, I'll open up in Maryland, my promise."

Aurelio recounts trying to stifle a laugh. He looked at Erik and with a blank look; Erik was also trying to keep his poker face. Finally, Erik spoke up.

"Jamie, we'll have ten agents by Monday morning."

True to their word, Meri, Erik, and Aurelio had ten agents by Monday... and 70+ fully licensed agents in their organization in less than a year! Dr. Meri and Erik were the number one recruiters in all of Experior in 2021, and the Experior presence in the U.S. was still a little bit like the Wild Wild West. To this day, Aurelio happily remembers how quickly Lee-Ann and I opened up Maryland for that team.

"You walk your talk, brother!" He tells me.

Shortly thereafter, more "Crazy Americans" called me up with some marketing ideas. Raza and Imrana Begg wanted me to waive the $150 start-up fee so that they could do a recruiting blitz in the States. This is something we have never done in eight years. They gave me details of the launch and I let the Beggs know that waiving those fees will cost Experior revenue, as those funds help fuel our massive technology, training, and software systems.

"Tell you what, Raza. I'll waive those fees if you bring in 40 agents this month."

"Done."

The Beggs didn't stop recruiting that month, and they didn't stop creatively marketing. They have developed a social media marketing system for their agents that drives leads to their teams, giving them the opportunity to prosper in personal production through organic, referral-based traffic as opposed to cold-calling, which most people rightfully despise. Not being a strong social media user myself, I hesitated when the Beggs ran their plans past me and Lee-Ann, but we remained open and flexible to their ideas, challenging them with goals that would motivate them to hit leaderboards, prosper, and have fun with the process.

Great leaders listen. Great leaders trust their team.

In business, there's a well-known problem of CEOs only having access to a fraction of the intel they need to run a business. Executive Coach Dawn Holly Johnson illustrates the Iceberg of Ignorance, a popular model coined in the 1980s by Sidney Yoshida.

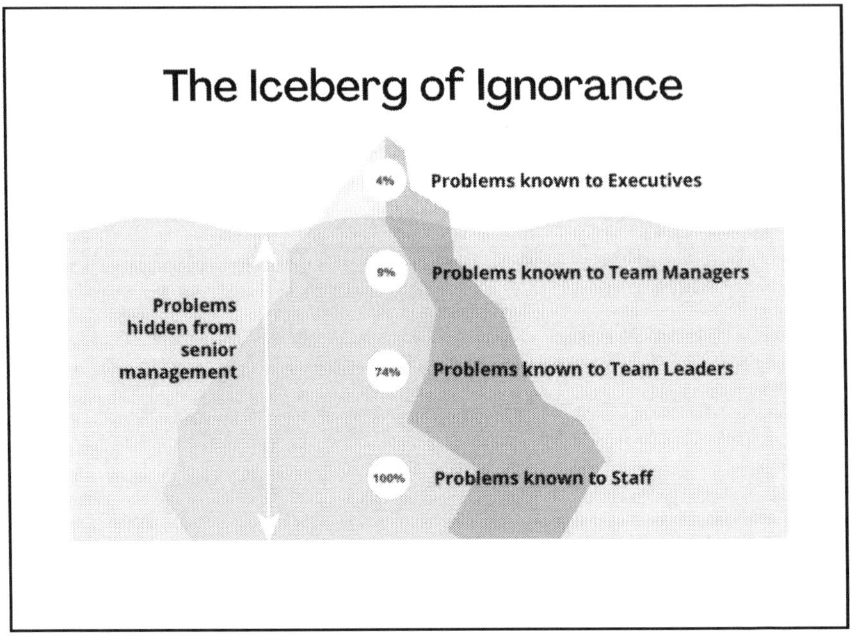

The Iceberg of Ignorance illustrates that management fails to understand an organization from the perspective of their customers, which may suppress company profits by as much as 40%, according to Johnson. If 100% of problems are apparent to a front-line worker, why are 96% percent of those problems filtered out before reaching the CEO and decision-makers of the organization?[3]

David Longmore will never forget the time when Experior was performing a logo change. I asked David one day, on an infamous contract delivery stop, if he'd provide some feedback and support on the logo change.

"Jamie, you're the CEO. What do you need me for?" He still fondly recalls how valued he felt when I solicited his support in that important decision.

3 Johnson, Dawn Holly. "What CEOs Need to Know". Page 53, Kindle. Copyright 2021 by Pierucci Publishing.

Darren Golka says that he can build with heart because he trusts Lee-Ann and me with our word, which is a far cry from the atmosphere he came from. When he came on board with Experior, one of his first questions was whether or not we could begin building in the United States.

"Absolutely, brother. We will make it happen one day." I literally got straight on the ball and began to learn about how Experior could operate in the United States.

Three years later, Golka has one of the biggest teams in the U.S.A. Stephen Covey calls this phenomenon the "Speed of Trust" in his book of the same name. When your team trusts you, they can build with heart, as Golka says. He knows he won't be taken advantage of; he can focus his life on changing the lives of others and supporting a strong team, the one he and his wife Stephanie call REOS, or; Recognize Each Other's Successes.

He tells his agents, "I'm not looking over my back, here. I'm free to build; nobody is going to steal my business away from me. With the Speed of Trust that Jamie and Lee-Ann have created, Stephanie and I are free to operate from abundance and grow at warp speed. That trust is the glue that holds everything together."

In your organization, can your agents, managers, and front-line staff freely illustrate the problems as well as their praises for the business? Are you intimidating your team? Do you say you have an open door, but you actually have your secretary filter out employee concerns before they reach you because you're too busy? Do you listen to your team? Can they call you, or does your gatekeeper prevent them from leveling with you, even when it hurts to know that you're falling short as a leader? Does your team make you a better leader? Do you allow them to do so?

Great Leadership Lessons:

#1. Great leaders listen and evolve with their teams.

#2. Great leaders have created an environment in which their team feels comfortable revealing the 96% of issues that are not traditionally heard by the CEOs of an organization.

Chapter Twelve

There's No Job Too Small for A Great Leader

"Gratitude is the aristocrat of all the emotions."
Bill Gove

Executive Director Henok Msghina loves to recall the story of a fateful Sunday night when one of our websites at Experior went down. Msghina was teaching a financial education class to some 75 students online. At the end of his lecture, he asked his students if they wanted to join a company where they could put their new skills into action. Over a dozen students jumped at the opportunity. The only problem? There was a website glitch that wasn't allowing Msghina to enroll his recruits.

Lee-Ann and I were at home that night; finally hearing the last of our sons' stereos turn off and putting up our feet after an eventful, noisy weekend in the Prickett household. At 10 p.m. Henok's time, which was midnight in Guelph, we get a text from Msghina:

> Jamie, the website's not working. I have a handful of students who want to join Experior, but there's a glitch. I know I can call broker support in the morning, but these folks are ready to enroll tonight...

I didn't bat an eyelash. Lee-Ann and I rolled up our sleeves, thanked Msghina for letting us know about the problem, and we cranked it out with our developers in the middle of the night. By we, I mean Lee-Ann. We weren't annoyed. Msghina had the opportunity to bring ten people into his organization that night, and we weren't going to let him down.

Msghina said, "Jamie, I'm so sorry. I know you're busy."

"Man, this is my job. This is what I live to do." A great leader is accessible, and there's no job too small. I'm happy our agents use my personal cell phone to let me know how I can help them. To me, it's an honor to have our agents trust us so much.

When David Longmore, a Jamaican immigrant who's had tremendous success with Experior, got promoted to Executive Director, I drove for an hour to congratulate him in person within 60 seconds of seeing the scoreboard. He hadn't even heard the good news himself by the time I arrived. I said, "David, check your text messages." His team was congratulating him. His mouth dropped.

"You drove all the way here to congratulate me?" Great leaders go the extra mile, literally.

Henok Msghina

Executive Director Rayon White loves to recall a time when Experior was still relatively new, and I'd make the trip from Guelph to Toronto weekly to deliver contracts to our agents. He'd razz me appreciatively, "Hey Jamie, you're the CEO. Can't you find somebody else or some service to do that for you?" The truth was, we were just in our third year when Rayon joined, and we were not in a financial position yet to hire all of the staff we needed. Lee-Ann and I had to take on every role in the company for a period of time. If you are too proud to be a janitor or a courier driver while building your business, then you've probably had far too many participation trophies in your lifetime. Great leaders get their hands dirty if it means getting the job done.

At the time, I didn't tell Rayon that Lee-Ann and I weren't just serving the food, but cooking it and doing the dishes, as well.

"Sure, I could hire somebody to deliver these contracts, Rayon. But then what excuse would I have for coming over here and kicking you guys into shape?" As silly as that may sound, there was truth in what I said. I'll never regret having to load up my backseat with stacks of contracts to hand-deliver to those agents, grabbing a few coffees on my way, and delivering the contracts to our agents in person. Those contracts represent the lives we change; the freedom we bring to our clients. There's nothing I would rather do more than celebrate with my teams on the business they closed and the people they'd blessed.

I've never been one of these CEOs who dresses the part, who has a sort of unapproachable air. I've been involved in companies where things would get quiet when the CEO entered the room. I like to think that in any room I enter, the volume goes up. People remember why we're here. They remember that it's okay to be themselves and fall on their faces because I've done that, too.

One of those moments during which you'd assume I'd put my best foot forward is during recruiting meetings. Hey, you want the guy at the helm to be polished, professional, and reliable, right? So dress the part? Not me. I don't want my polish to shine through, I want my scars. I want people to know that I've been to war, and I have the scars to prove it. Sometimes it turns people off, but time and again they'll come to understand that this approachability is what makes them successful and, in turn, me and Lee-Ann.

There has been more than one occasion where I've shown up to woo somebody to our team in sweaty gym clothes or in the middle of the night in a hotel ambush like I did with Dianne and Francis Sinday. Great leaders don't need to hide behind fancy suits. A lot of that posturing and peacocking comes from manipulation, not motivation. I am not saying to never dress nice, but sometimes you've gotta let your hair down.

Beyond that, great leaders are servants. In January 2021, I met Dr. Meri Robinson, Erik Robinson, and Aurelio Evans for the first time on a Zoom call. Within just two months, Dr. Meri and Erik, eagerly recruiting a U.S. Experior team, asked me if they could do a March Madness recruiting event. I had built trust with them in a short period of time, so I handed them the reins and said, "whatever you guys need, count me in. I'm there."

"Alright, Jamie. What's the most anybody has ever recruited in this company in a month?"

"Thirty or so," I said.

"So, we're gonna double that, Jamie. And then we're going to reward those 50 or so new recruits with a 'Dinner with the CEO.' Are you okay with that?" How could I say no? I love when my team gets creative with marketing, and I wanted Dr. Meri, Erik, and Aurelio to function in their most elevated capacity: which is recruiting like mad with fun, community-building events.

Sure enough, they recruited over 50 people, and that night I sent a $50 gift card to at least 60 people. That March Madness event became the single most important recruiting event for Experior Financial Group in the United States. Each individual who won that dinner - which ended up being a full night of playing games, laughing, and learning together - was allowed to bring one guest.

But they didn't have me stop there. They were going to test and see how Lee-Ann and I would show up for them as leaders.

One day, Erik called me and said, "Jamie, the U.S. market is new. Things are different here than they are in Canada. Dr. Meri and I are new, as well. We're going to need more mentorship than other agents who've been in the industry for 20 or 30 years."

I didn't skip a beat. I committed to being Dr. Meri, Erik, and Aurelio's personal coach once weekly, as well as training their team twice weekly during both a morning and an evening session. Their leaders showed up and they've already had an agent crossing a $100,000 after only six months. Darren Golka showed up for our United States team as well, also spending one-on-one time nurturing and training the Maryland Team weekly.

Dr. Meri and Erik continued to push throughout 2021 to see where Lee-Ann and I would meet them; they kept calling Lee-Ann and me not just to show up as mentors, not just to show up on Zoom, but to literally fly across North America to support their new team. We packed up our passports, even when it wasn't easy.

Dr. Meri and Erik Robinson

One time Dr. Meri and Erik had arranged a conference in Texas to celebrate the new agents they'd recruited there. They asked Lee-Ann and me to fly in. There were a few hiccups to that plan, however. First, we were worried about crossing the border to the U.S.; this was during the height of lockdowns all over North America. Secondly, a few days before this event, we had not one but *two* Mercedes vehicles stolen from our driveway.

Erik still laughs about the day we finally made it to Texas. We drove all the way from Guelph, Ontario to Dallas in the brand-new Bentley SUV we had picked up just two days prior. The air conditioning went out on that trip when I ran over a truck tire -

you know, the tread that transport trucks shed sometimes - and in case you hadn't heard, it gets hot on those plains driving through the Midwestern United States. Any event these incredible leaders are throwing is going to be a success and a lot of fun, but this was a weekend I'll never forget. For two nights straight, Takiyah, Lee-Ann, myself, Dr. Meri, and Erik stayed up playing board games until 4 a.m. together. On the second night, I looked at Erik and said, "you're forever going to be The Crazy Americans team in my book."

"We're crazy? You've got your family here in a Presidential Suite at this hotel. You drove twenty-something hours from Canada and you're sitting here playing board games with us instead of having caviar and filet mignon at the Ritz. Who's crazy?" I love that our love for our team is disarming.

"We live to serve!" I told Erik.

Well, he took me literally that night. A few months later Dr. Meri and Erik decided to throw yet another event. This one was going to be a presentation to potential new recruits in their business and a friend's restaurant opening. There were some logistics to handle, but somehow, we made it and so did my remarkable wife. When we arrived, Dr. Meri said, "I have a crazy idea, Jamie. Why don't you, me, Erik, and Lee-Ann serve the food?" I didn't know then that the restaurant didn't actually have servers yet. That's the night that Lee-Ann and I weren't just the President and CEOs featured at an event, but we got to show this new team that we are servant leaders, in the most literal way. I treasure the fact that several dozen people's first impression of me and Lee-Ann was serving them. Because that's who we are. That's what we do. We live for these agents. If only we could serve every single new recruit we bring on just so that it's explicitly clear: we're here for *you*.

Serving new friends at a recruiting event put on by Dr. Meri and Erik Robinson (not pictured)

What would you do if you got that middle-of-the-night text from Henok? Would you have pretended you didn't see it until the morning? Would you have told your agent that your phone was on Airplane Mode? Would you have snapped back, "it's a weekend at midnight, are you insane?" Do you invest time in celebrating your team? Are you "too good" to support your team? Or are you so good that your team can rely on you anytime, day or night? Do you want to hide out in your presidential suite ordering caviar and champagne? Or do you love to commiserate and bond with your team? Is your team like family? Do you want them to be your servants, or do you live to serve your team?

Great Leadership Lessons:

#1. Great leaders don't require of others what they themselves won't do.

#2. Great leaders sometimes take the role of chief cook and bottle washers. There's no job too small when you're building a great organization.

Chapter Thirteen

Great Leaders Inspire Others

"Life isn't about finding yourself. It's about creating yourself."
George Bernard Shaw

When I met Frank De Lio, he was getting beat up in his old company, where we both worked. He admits that deep down, he had imposter syndrome; he didn't feel worthy of the accolades he received in that business. And how could he? At the top of his game after years of building his organization, his family didn't have real security. They were still cautious with money. One night, when he began checking out Experior, I told him, "Frank, you're gonna make a million dollars a year in no time."

"I love your enthusiasm brother, but I'm not so sure. Let's see what happens." At his current pace, it would be hard for Frank *not* to make a million dollars a year, and I will put it out there right now, but before he crosses year eight with us, he will be over that threshold. After all, he crushed through $500,000 a year in five and a half years. Now, with some compounding, hmmmmm... He remembers that night when I told him, "Frank, you're going to change 10,000 lives. And with Experior, you're finally gonna get paid to do so."

At that moment, Frank shifted from hope to hustle. He made over $200,000 his first year, and he started to believe me. Then $300,000, and he believed me a little more. Now, he's at over half a million dollars a year, and I asked Frank; what changed?

"I believe in myself," was what he said. After sucking wind with the Practice Company for a decade and getting scammed by our first business partners when we went out on our own, why did we keep going? In short, we were **positively brainwashed.** We were dreamers.

The Bible says that without vision, the people will perish. What Lee-Ann and I dreamt about was a company that was so full of integrity that the agents could make more than the owners. Not the shareholders, not the corporate bigwigs, and not the VCs, but the agents.

Experior Executive Director Tzachi Chen says that there's a compounding effect when you don't give up. Your playing small doesn't serve the world. It keeps you playing small.

Just like the hare in the story I told you about in Chapter One, the Goliath you learned about in Chapter Four gets lazy, cocky, over-confident, and eventually, he tires. Being born with natural talent never, ever outpaces consistent hard work.

It hasn't been easy to put my name on this book because anybody who works with me knows that I don't want the glory. I merely shine the light on my team.

Dr. Meri and Erik Robinson, my "Crazy Americans," developed a remarkable system for their new recruits who have different products, different markets, and different business structures than our Canadian counterparts. They call it the Green Sheet.

With Dr. Meri having her doctorate in education and Erik having over 20 years of experience in selling anything from clean energy to cars, they are uniquely qualified to bring their selling systems to the table, despite being less than a year old with Experior. One day, I began using Dr. Meri and Erik's 1-2-3 Selling System called the Green Sheet as part of our Experior training program. I didn't try to rewrite or rebrand it and call it my own, as I'd seen too many leaders before me do. I made sure that the creators of the system received recognition for bringing their inspiring system to us.

Erik and Dr. Meri are excellent at inspiring new recruits to dream big about what they can do with Experior and this brand-new U.S. market. On the ground floor of a new business, the opportunity for their new agents is limitless. I've often told my team that I wish I'd been with my practice company on the ground floor. I'd have been earning millions a year as opposed to struggling for a decade. Frank, Mauro, and Laval would have, too. But the opportunity is different here.

To inspire others and as a nod to our board game habit, Erik has an elegant way of making the opportunity simple to inspire his new recruits.

He says, "Who Wants to Be a Millionaire? Look, if you had joined a company that currently has fifty or a hundred thousand agents in the beginning, you'd have the opportunity of a lifetime. But the world has changed, and so has our industry."

Leaders need to be at the forefront of these changes. Goliaths don't want to change. They'd rather not ruffle any feathers and just keep it the way it is. To me, rewarding our agents with the single greatest compensation plan is a no-brainer. The agents are the ones that make the company. Sure, you can try to nickel and dime folks, but then turnover is horrendous. You might ask, what if I treat them well and train them so well, and they leave. Well, I think that's better than not treating them well and training them well, and they stay.

Sometimes, inspiring others doesn't come from having complex processes and algorithms. Sometimes it comes from something as simple as systematizing a selling tool in a 1-2-3 process, such as Dr. Meri and Erik have done. Sometimes, it comes from simply showing people that they no longer have to worry about losing their business or income when a company sells, as had happened to Dr. Meri and Erik in the past. Sometimes, it comes from simply asking the question, "who wants to be a millionaire?" and allowing that person to craft a life that doesn't just make it possible for them, but makes it fun, too.

Great Leadership Lessons:

#1: Great leaders inspire others.

#2: Inspiring others doesn't have to be complex; sometimes people are most inspired not by numbers, figures, and formulas, but by knowing that their dreams can be materialized with ease.

Part Three

Keys To Creating a Great Company

Chapter Fourteen

Create a Great Company with Equal Opportunities for All

"All of us do not have equal talent, but all of us should have an equal opportunity to develop our talent."
John F Kennedy

"Venture capitalists will tell you that they'd rather buy a great team than a great idea."
Joe Kraus- Cofounder, Excite

As the title of this book suggests, Lee-Ann and I started at ground zero when building Experior Financial Group. We've built a great company with a great team that's determined, motivated, hopeful, and happy. In Part Three of You Can't Fall Off The Floor, you're going to learn from our team members' stories about what we've done to allow our Great Leaders to build a Great Company.

If you've struggled to allow a certain level of success and abundance into your life, at the risk of sounding like a total hippie, I'll suggest that it's because you're letting something hold you back. That something is generally one of two things: a) a limiting belief, or b) imposter syndrome.

A limiting belief is just what it sounds like. A belief that you hold about your worth, your potential, or your abilities. Zig Ziglar calls it the Do-Have-Be. You believe that you've got to *do* the thing before you can *have* the glory so that you can *be* happy.

Imposter syndrome is another big enemy of success. It's the false notion that you don't deserve your divine inheritance, your birthright, and/or your status as the king or queen you are. You are afraid that if and when you succeed, you'll be discovered as a fraud or imposter. Sheryl Sandburg popularized this notion in her book "Lean In" when she admitted that, although the Facebook team sought her leadership as their COO, she was subconsciously waiting for the day that they'd learn she was just a fraud - that she wasn't as good as other people in her position - generally men. She asks readers to take their seat at the table in the most memorable story in an otherwise pretty unmemorable book.

Great companies decimate imposter syndrome. We don't fill people up with false hopes and facades, but we surgically extract the magic gift that each individual who onboards with us has within them. We shine the light on that gift that so many kings and queens who've joined us have always had, but hadn't fully realized. In a great company, there is equal opportunity for all.

In this book, you've read the stories of over a dozen individuals who've floundered in previous companies. Rayon Whyte is no dummy, but he struggled for ten years in his previous company. God bless his incredible wife and family for believing in him. Daniel Prete struggled so hard in his last position that it brought both him and his mentor, Mauro, to tears. Frank De Lio never broke past the $160,000 income level until he'd been at his former company for 16, and it certainly wasn't for lack of trying, nor a lack of innate talent. The man's a genius. It took him just five and a half years to create $500,000 in annual income at Experior.

So why do so many men and women join a great company and thrive where, in other companies, they floundered?

A great company is designed to honor the individual.

The public-school systems in North America certainly don't honor the unique individual; they honor a single way of doing and being, and it causes otherwise brilliant kids to struggle. Perhaps I was one of them, but I've never thought I was brilliant. Just determined.

Your mechanic may be just as smart as your doctor; one of them just took a different direction in their career. When I'm hiring anybody from employees to entrepreneurs, I look for one critical quality that is tragically and vastly overlooked by other leaders. It's the quality of followship that I briefly mentioned in Part Two.

Rayon Whyte shared with me one day that he's never read so much in his life. He struggled hard for his first ten years in this industry, but when he joined Experior, he learned that he's damn smart. We unlocked his divine essence; he's intelligent, kind, compassionate, and he's a remarkable leader.

How do you look for team members with great followship? How do you give this opportunity to people who have never been honored, adored, and respected the way we love our team?

Look for language patterns that illustrate a person's mindset.

Followship signs include great listening skills, humility, and personal responsibility. I'd rather somebody admit that they're wrong any day than hear somebody say "yeah, I know" when given direction. I'd rather have somebody say, "no, I don't understand that. Will you elaborate?" than somebody who says, "of course I understand. Here's why I'm right." These know-it-alls aren't just a bummer to work with; they're dangerous.

In my previous business, I was a know-it-all. I was blue-pilled, brainwashed - I'd drunk the Kool-Aid. If you weren't for me, you were against me. I lacked understanding for anybody who didn't see my way of thinking.

Among the many qualities I've tempered over the past eight years, it's my ability to have grace for others that I've tempered the most. But when it comes to building a great company, I look for great followers, not know-it-alls.

Equal Opportunity for Immigrants

Intelligence is not the dominant trait of a leader. Education doesn't correlate with wealth. A lot of people wax poetic about equality, but here at Experior, we've learned that it's not enough to wave a colorful flag and subsidize a few people in each department to promote diversity. A great company doesn't look for advanced degrees or pedigrees, they look for team members who are rich in passion and bred with strong hearts. A great company is built not with a gaggle of exhausted parts, but with a strong, connected unit.

Periodically I see people get frustrated with immigrants who speak in broken English, which perplexes me to no end. These people came to live in a foreign place. Most of them came because they want to work hard and provide a better opportunity for their family. They had the courage to leave what was familiar to them, and they speak at least two languages. To people who are critical of immigrants, I like to point out that they're probably a lot smarter than me or you. In our company, it's proven to be true time and time again.

In a great company, there is truly equal opportunity for everybody to succeed - but I'm not just ruffling feathers for the camera. I've put my money where my mouth is, and in the following stories, you'll see how dozens of agents in my business have become statistical outliers in their success.

People have joked that Experior looks like the United Nations. It's true, especially in comparison with so many companies whose leadership is pale, stale, and male. Experior has achieved success by accepting and celebrating people from all countries and walks of life.

Tzachi Chen loves to call Head Office and say, "Hey, who speaks 'X' language, I want this client to feel completely comfortable." In my experience, we've never failed to procure an agent who speaks just about every language imaginable.

Tzachi is a Canadian immigrant from Israel who arrived speaking barely a dozen words in English. When he came to Canada, his wife was pregnant with their second child, and they were penniless. It didn't change fast. He worked in the industry but made so little money that his wife would bury a few dollars away here and there from her job; worried that they would have to stow away back to Israel at some point; with or without Tzachi.

From left to right: Tzachi Chen, Dror David and Asaf Halperin (Executive Director and David's recruiter)

Like so many stories you've read in this book, I ambushed Tzachi at a coffee shop. I showed up at a meeting where Tzachi mistakenly thought he was going to meet with me to recruit me to his former company. Tzachi tells me that what attracted him to Experior was the fact that we're a ground floor business; he had the opportunity to start afresh somewhere. After slamming through his personal contacts in just a week, Tzachi worried that in order to see success, he'd have to become a workaholic. But today, Tzachi earns over $100,000 in passive income and more than triple what he used to earn. He loves to remind our immigrant agents that, in 2005, he came here with nothing, but his kids will be millionaires. He'll retire in less than ten years after starting with our business in 2016.

He's not unlike Bhupinder Cheema from India, who reminds us that he used to walk seven kilometers to school and dream of having a car as he and his friends would watch cars drive on the roads past them. Sadly, Cheema lost his father at eight years old, and in his teens began working as a mechanic. There, he met a financial planner who introduced Bhupinder to the industry of financial services and taking care of families. Still feeling the stress on his family of losing his dad so young, Bhupinder wanted to devote his life to protecting families' incomes and came to us by way of England. Today, Bhupinder leads an organization of over 400 licensed agents.

Also motivated by transforming families is Madhab Dulal, originally from Nepal. In 2008, Dulal left his job at a grocery store and immigrated to Canada where he was delighted to make $50,000 annually in a Walmart warehouse. After two and a half years, he found that he would cap out at $70,000 annually if he'd become a manager in the warehouse; this was his "Canadian dream."

Dulal later left that job and spent several years with another financial service company. Being obsessively devoted to delivering financial freedom for clients, Dulal couldn't move forward with this company where he only had one carrier's products to promote. Sometime during my editing of this book, Dulal hit $250,000 in annual income with Experior... after only two years with us. I called him up and asked him how it felt. He said, "What felt better than hitting two-fifty was that one of my teammates, Prakash Bashyal, hit $100,000 thousand on the same day."

"So, what's your next big goal, Madhab?" I asked.

"Jamie, once I hit a million dollars, I'm writing my book too."

"You better believe I'll buy the first thousand copies, brother."

Speaking of guys who should write a book, Denesh Logeswaran has seen his share of gunfire. His parents fled Sri Lanka as refugees after witnessing bombs and war. They were able to become Canadian citizens, but they didn't come here with money.

As we learned in Part One, Denesh was caught in the crossfire of gang violence and got shot twice in the back. In his twenties, he worked for $12.75 in a warehouse. He felt like a slave working nine-to-five. When he was told that there was hope, that he could become a forklift operator and make a full $2 more per hour, he was done. It's one thing to work hard, but another to feel like you're dead inside to do it.

Denesh Logeswaran

After a couple of years of grinding in a warehouse, he met Andrea Rogers, a woman so passionate and purpose-driven that she can melt anybody's heart and give anybody the ability to believe in themselves. Rogers became Denesh's mentor and picked up where his grandfather had left off in teaching him about entrepreneurship, himself a car parts salesman. Denesh was eager to make his grandfather proud.

Even though his grandfather had since died of prostate cancer, Denesh felt that his natural proclivity to business ownership came from the man he admired so much. He often fondly recalls the moment when he fractured his arm falling from a slide at the playground. His grandfather grabbed Denesh with one hand and the tricycle with another and walked home. It was not long after that that he found out his grandfather was in severe pain at the time due to his cancer.

"Andrea, nobody will trust me selling financial stuff; a guy who's been shot and who grew up on the wrong side of the tracks." Rogers let Denesh know that rather than focus on his past, he ought to focus on the thousands of immigrant families who have virtually no financial education that he would help. In the company where Andrea and Denesh started, he made $14,000 during his highest income year, and he was there for eight years. Today, he's making over $100,000 annually and will surely be at over $200,000 in the next few months. When asked how he overcame the self-doubt of being a punk turned financial advisor, he responds, "My new life and wealth attract others." Like Madhab Dulal, Denesh has found prosperity in becoming the magnet.

Tariq Ba'Aqeel is originally from Saudi Arabia but grew up in the hood of Toronto. He, like Denesh, lamented the lack of understanding among immigrant families and worried that he was doomed to mediocrity because of having grown up on the wrong side of the tracks. He points out that so many immigrants come from cash-based societies. His wife Sophie, now joining Tariq in the business, points out that she found, as an immigrant from Cambodia, that immigrants subconsciously hold limiting beliefs that come from the visual representation around you of all of the brown and black people struggling. She points out that immigrant families have negative beliefs around money, saying that "it doesn't grow on trees" and "life is hard."

"Being an immigrant is tough," she says, "but largely because we inherit this anxiety about life from parents who went through hell to bring us here. Tariq and I are here because we have to show people that it's possible when you believe in yourself and the service you're providing. For us, that's providing people with financial freedom; we live for that." Today, they earn over $200,000 annually with Experior.

The Ba'Aqeel Family

Editha Ramil also came here with little more than hope. She worked as a nanny in 2004, leaving her four children behind while she worked towards a better life than they had in the Philippines. She had worked as a pharmacist in the Philippines. She remembers when her sister called and said, "You're heading to Canada to work as a caregiver when here in the Philippines you have two nannies? What are you thinking?"

Editha and Wilson Ramil

From 2004 to 2009, Editha worked along, eventually settling in Alberta where she saw more opportunity. She was fueled by the naysayers who said she needed to give up and come home. During those five years, she only saw her family twice. She worked in a hospital, Subway restaurant, and cleaned houses. Finally, she was hired in Alberta at the University as a pharmacy assistant, but she still lived paycheck to paycheck. When she got into finance in 2010, her company promised her the moon. They said, "You'll make $100,000 a year if you just take this exam."

Nine years later, Ramil was a Senior Marketing Director with her company and would have been an executive or CEO level director soon, but she wasn't even making enough to buy a house. With her family now living in the United States, she yearned to work in a business where she could enjoy time with them. When she evaluated the possibility of moving to Experior, she made it clear that she wanted to be paid for her value. She knew her worth coming in. In just two years since 2019, Ramil is earning $200,000 a year, on her way to $300,000 soon.

She loves to tell her team: "If your plan doesn't work, change the plan, not the goal." Her husband, Wilson Ramil, has now joined her in the business - another inspiring story of husband-and-wife teams in our agency.

Fellow immigrant David Longmore remembers coming to Canada from Jamaica looking for work. Once, he took a job moving furniture for an Italian family. He says it felt like he had emptied Buckingham Palace before they were done. Another time he was directed to cut a tree down... with an ax. He laughs about it today and says, "I just put $30,000 into renovations in my home and we didn't even think about it."

His good friend Rayon Whyte, also from Jamaica, only made $28,000 a year with his previous company in financial services. He was beholden to one product. Today, he, too, is designing his ideal home. When sharing home remodeling stories with David Longmore, Whyte began weeping.

He says, "I can't believe how good God is. My life has changed in every way, in every positive way."

Funnily enough, it all started when Frank De Lio showed up at Whyte's door, hoping to recruit him into the industry. He did, but his wife said, "If you don't make this work, I'll divorce you." Seeing how happy Rayon and his wife are after 38 years of marriage, that's hard to believe. But De Lio made good on his promise to Whyte's family. He brought Rayon to Experior, and he's more than made up for the time he lost in the Practice Company. He says, "my kids call him Uncle Frank, and he calls me his black son from Italy." Whatever they call each other, I'm just glad we brought Rayon and his family home to Experior.

From Left to Right: David Longmore, Martinna Bowen (one of Mauro Arturi's agents), and Rayon Whyte

When Neela Mannan came to Canada from Dubai, she had worked as a business professional and immediately began working with a financial services company, just ten days after stepping foot in Canada. Her marriage struggled and the divorce dragged on for two years. In 2016, she came to see me. She was exhausted but still had hope. She hated the situation in her life but loved the industry.

I asked Neela why she wanted to join us. She had seen Frank De Lio come from another company to build Experior and she'd heard rumors that her clients would be better off, her team would be better off, and ultimately, her family would be better off.

To this day, Neela has to grab a tissue to tell this story, but after 15 years of struggle in the industry, she finally had to sell her most prized possession; jewelry she'd come here with from Dubai. Jewelry is a big deal in Dubai, and she had earmarked some of those pieces to give to her daughters or grandkids.

Neela Mannan and her daughter, Maysoon

I once asked her if she feels better now about selling the jewelry as now she can buy it all back, and more. She says that she has an even better legacy to leave her kids and grandkids. She can show them a woman who never gave up; a woman who started a business with Experior at nearly 60 years old in 2016 and created a legacy for her family. Her daughter now works in her business with her.

She said, "This is a dream come true."

Chapter Fifteen

Create a Great Company as a Family

"There is no such thing as a self-made man.
You will reach your goals only with the help of others."
George Shinn

"I always say I'm not going to work; I'm going to play with my friends."
Brian Tyree Henry

"So do you miss home?" I found myself asking Executive Director Adeola Abiodun one day. Adeola comes to us from a previous company where he had an organization of 34 agents. He smiled big and laughed. "Jamie, I have hundreds of family members with Experior! I *am* home!"

Tyrone and Melissa Hinds; Neela and Maysoon Mannan; Editha and Wilson Ramil; Dr. Meri and Erik Robinson; Darren and Stephanie Golka; Tariq and Sophie Ba'Aqeel; Francis and Dianne Sinday; and Lee-Ann and myself - we all have this in common, along with so many others: *we've made prosperity a family affair.*

Darren Golka likes to say that although the numbers intrigued him (we spent hours in conference rooms and weeks working to attract him to our business when he was ready to give the entire industry the boot), it was the relationship I have with Lee-Ann that gave him and his wife Stephanie the knowledge in their hearts that the move to Experior was right for them.

More importantly, Darren is not shy about saying, "It was Stephanie who had the final word. She felt good about who you and Lee-Ann were as a couple. We could see that you were a man of integrity by the way you treated Lee-Ann." I feel honored to hear those words, especially since Lee-Ann literally kicked me under the table during my first meeting with Golka and some of his top advisors. I think that, by integrity, what he meant to say is, "I talk too fast to keep up with myself if I was lying, and Lee-Ann is a saint." No wonder Stephanie was so enthusiastic about joining us!

I feel a lot of pride in the immigrants who've found success with our company. I feel equally excited about how many men and women have found the chance to spend more meaningful time with their families since joining Experior. I love to know that Madhab Dulal spends every morning reading books with his son and each evening spending quality time with his younger child, his daughter. I love to know that Tasso Lagos is looking forward to crossing over to the $250,000 income level, but still has the time and energy to put all four of his children to bed and wake up with them each morning instead of spending several days a week traveling.

He says of his business, "My team is like McDonald's; we're in the real estate business. I'm focusing more on recruiting than serving individual clients transactionally so that I can build more passive income and spend free time with my family."

Madhab Dulal

Sophie Ba'Aqeel says that, in her Cambodian culture, parents go to Temple to read their childrens' futures and see their destinies. Her parents learned when Sophie was a girl that she would meet her true love at the age of 27, get married, become very wealthy, and change the world together. She says that when her son was born, it was like going to a confirmation when they brought him to an Experior convention.

"This is your family, little one," she says to her son, who's been to nearly every Experior event since his birth.

Raza and Imrana Begg love to remind new agents they recruit that Experior Financial Group gives them the opportunity to homeschool their children and never miss a day in their children's lives. Although they've become the number one personal producer (they're a husband-and-wife team who share the same code) in our entire company, Raza and Imrana have taken four or five family vacations since joining us in 2021, which is six months ago at the time of writing this book. They've taken their children to visit family, to Las Vegas, and even to Disneyworld. When Imrana is taking care of the kids and needs a break, Raza can step away from the business easily for the afternoon to make sure that his wife can recharge. Experior Financial Group is proud to see so many families thriving because of the freedom and flexibility our agents have in their businesses.

Probably the most breathtaking story of family comes from Mario Francella, who suffered kidney failure at ten years old that landed him in a children's hospital with a 10% chance of living from a disease called hydronephrosis. Sick Kids is where they send children who are seriously ill, which I learned when my own son Addison was there in the story that I recounted in Chapter Four. Francella spent four years of his life in that hospital, from ages ten to fourteen. Not only did he have multiple surgeries and procedures during that time, but he watched 47 other kids pass away. He still has tattoos of the names of those he became friends with on his arm.

Somehow, Mario healed, and at 14 he was allowed to leave the hospital. The problem was that Mario hadn't just lost his childhood and watched most of his friends die for four years, but his parents lost their dream home funding his stay in the hospital.

He remembers sitting in his room listening to them fight one day about money. He realized that all the insurance they had purchased through their financial advisor wasn't covering the expenses from the hospital. Knowing his dad had worked seven days a week to have that home broke Mario's heart. To add insult to injury, his brother looked at him and said, "We're losing everything because of you."

That summer, not wanting to add any more burden to the family, Mario told his parents that he'd be staying with a friend. He told the friend that his parents got a condo in Florida and that they'd be there for the summer. Long story short, Mario wouldn't be a burden to anybody that summer because he was homeless, under the bridge at Lake Shore and Spadina in Downtown Toronto. In three days, Mario had lost everything he'd brought with him.

Another individual who was there took Francella under his wing a little.

He said, "You have three options. You can sell drugs, you can rob and steal, or you can become a squeegee kid." Mario chose the latter and stole a squeegee from a gas station the next day. Well, apparently, he chose both of the latter two options. He filled something that resembled a bucket he'd found with water at Lake Shore and began running up to cars. He says that it breaks his heart to see kids doing that today; he wonders who they are, where they're from, and what drove them to the streets.

He used his clever wit to attract people that summer. They'd pull up and he'd feign a look at a watch that didn't exist on his wrist and say, "Hey, look at you! You're right on time! Shall I start with the front window or the back?" Or he'd hold up a sign that said, "I'm not homeless, I'm an entrepreneur and this is my squeegee business." The more he made people smile, the easier it got to turn twenty cents into fifty, and then into one, two, or three dollars.

Mario didn't return home when summer ended, spending a little over a year on the streets. When it got particularly cold or hot, he'd stay in a sort of halfway house that was essentially a drug den. He remembers a black and white TV show that played the Cooking Channel. He'd watch families gathering around a good meal and thought: *I'm gonna be a chef.*

Mario Francella

He went back to his parent's house and made amends, but the next day he began knocking on the doors of every single restaurant he could to see who would give him a job. After he was called out of dishwashing to cook food a few times when the chefs didn't show up, he snuck his way into becoming a chef. He didn't just flip burgers, Francella eventually became one of the youngest executive chefs in Toronto. He won cooking competitions across

Canada and even developed a successful catering business. He knocked on between 60 and 100 doors a day to get his name out there and made six figures at 20 years old. He thought he had the life of his dreams; a great condo, a great car, and a great girlfriend, but he knew nothing about business and didn't pay any taxes. Soon, he lost everything, joking that everything got repossessed, including the girlfriend.

That's when a friend of his said, "Come work for me in financial services for the summer." Mario struggled for 15 years in the insurance industry, but finally found a home with Experior. He bought his parents a retirement home, a gift that brought his life full circle. He now says that Experior is his family; he's experienced more love, acceptance, and encouragement from this company than he's ever experienced in his life; and he doesn't have to work until 2 a.m. in front of a hot grill to live his dream life. He's finally home.

Chapter Sixteen

Create a Great Company with Continually Evolving Products

"Do not follow where the path may lead. Go instead where there is no path and leave a trail."
Ralph Waldo Emerson

One of the biggest complaints I get when the fish "jump in our boat" as Mauro Arturi quipped to the attorneys during our infamous lawsuit, is that they don't evolve their products or business model.

If every fast-food chain on the planet can serve meatless options, every junk food purveyor can come up with a gluten-free option to add to their suite of offerings; if your local coffee shop can carry 25 unique vegan drink options; if Silicon Valley can adjust technology every three minutes to meet the demands of users; if hundreds of thousands of people worldwide can move towards progressive, decentralized, digital currencies: why can't you continually evolve your products?

Executive Director Daniel Prete spent eight years with another company where he was limited to what he calls "1970s financial instruments." In today's world, he has the opportunity to help clients create wealth and financial stability through a huge assortment of insurance and investment products. Prete identifies as "infinite banking" through certain life insurance products. There are well-established insurance vehicles that allow our clients to grow millions upon millions of dollars completely tax-free.

Prete doesn't cold call or go to networking events. He doesn't run traffic to his social media pages or advertise on his local grocer's shopping carts. Prete is 33 years old and he's 100% referral-based in his business. If you've toiled in sales praying for new leads and cold-calling until your jaw locks at the end of the week, you understand how remarkable it is to be 100% referral-based as a young agent in any industry. Experior has allowed Prete to serve his clients with a suite of products that is so vast that he can truly do best by the client. Why doesn't every insurance company or agent in the world offer continually evolving products?

Perhaps it's laziness. We've chosen to broker just about everything on the market, not just the products that we're incentivized to sell through our corporation. Raza Begg has been in the industry since 2008, but he loves the environment of abundance and ease that Lee-Ann and I have created when it comes to what products our agents use. He used to feel pressure to sell certain company's products, but today he loves to say that, "Jamie lets me do the right thing for my clients. I never feel pressured to do anything else."

Not only do we continually evolve our business, but our agents are the benefactors of every single change or improvement we make. When Tasso Lagos came to this country, he worked in restaurants. His wife got sick, and he found himself working two jobs to support her while she was sick. 12 months after her diagnosis, Tasso had depleted his savings and maxed out his credit cards. When she died 18 months after their wedding, he was weeks away from selling their house. One of her cousins created a GoFundMe for illnesses and final expenses, and Tasso was disappointed that nobody had talked to him about finances when he could have insured himself and his wife against illness, disability, and loss of life. Today, when people listen to his story, he feels blessed to turn that painful experience into something that will bless and prosper others.

From Left to Right: Tasso Lagos, Delroy Peart (Tasso and Myron's Executive Director), and Myron Weekes

Tariq Ba'Aqeel had a turning point moment similar to Daniel Prete when working with a large bank. He chose, one day, to give a client some coaching on how to build credit. He was taken into a side room and berated by his manager for trying to help somebody. He was even given a written warning. He was told that his job is to hit targets, not educate customers. Unless that customer was going to apply for a loan or overdraft protection, Tariq was told that helping people wasn't his job. Today, Tariq is recognized in the top ten agents in Experior year after year and even took home the number one spot in 2020. Once Tariq was given the freedom to help clients, he prospered, and so did those clients.

He loves to recall a story of a woman he met in her thirties who was turned down by several advisors because she didn't have money to invest. But she needed help: She was in massive debt, mostly from student loans, and recently diagnosed with breast cancer. The woman was willing to do what it took to get on track, but without money to invest, most agents and advisors looked at her like that bank did; as worthless.

She's a single mom, diagnosed with breast cancer, buried in student loans, and on a reduced income from disability. Tariq sat down with her and came up with a plan. They reprioritized her debt and reduced it from fourteen to three years, without taking additional money from what she was already paying in something called a debt snowballing technique. She's now debt-free with an emergency savings account and finally planning for retirement. Tariq recalls the moment he presented this plan to his client. They were both in tears with joy that she could find freedom from a situation that looked impossible to manage.

Tariq isn't just a great coach and advisor, but he's a participant in products that have kept him and his wife in a financially stable situation. Tariq is autistic, and when his son was born, he decided to purchase a specific health insurance product that would cover the costs of occupational therapists and treatment in case his son presented as autistic. Sure enough, the boy did present as autistic at four years old. Tariq and his wife Sophie received the money needed to support their son because of the critical illness insurance he had on his son. His claim paid his family $100,000 to help the family out.

Today, Tariq and Sophie are leaders in the Canadian autistic community, helping other parents protect their families if their children present as autistic, which generally doesn't occur until after the toddler years. Because of great insurance agents like Tariq and Sophie, those parents can focus on being present with their children, not working fourteen-hour days to support the care their kids need from therapists. Because of the work agents like Tariq and Sophie do, children will get what they truly need when they're sick: more time with their families.

Darren Golka... man, when I got a call from him and hit Google, my heart skipped a beat just a little. He's a legend in the industry. He's not a small guy. I knew his organization would be massive.

He started the call by saying, "Hey, Jamie. Before I get started, just a little bit about me. I love the book *The Coach*. Secondly, I come from a company where I sold term insurance probably 80% of the time."

To neutralize my nerves from having been caught off guard at the beginning of the call, I immediately spat out, "Oh, so you mean to tell me that you were only a total crook 20% of the time." This was clearly a joke, and he understood what I was saying since the Practice Company I worked at for ten years only sold term life insurance. We were brainwashed to believe that anything other than term is evil. That took me a few years to have the Kool-Aid wear off, and I knew that Darren was, in fact, a great agent.

This brought Darren and me to a level of brothers and peers. Nobody was interviewing anybody anymore. We were just sharing. And the "crook" thing lasted for months as a great inside joke. But there's really no such thing as joking, right? Everything we say, everything, has an element of truth to it. I'd like to think that at that moment I reached out and extended a hand to Darren, saying, "Yeah man, this industry has some shady folks. So, let's Robin Hood this puppy together."

Darren Golka and me working in my office.

Oh, and I'll tell you what, Darren is getting a good chuckle about that last paragraph, not just remembering the crook comment or the effortless camaraderie that ensued the first time he and Stephanie came to our home for dinner from all the way across the country a few weeks later, but also, alas, another inside joke. It feels apt to share since I clearly have no shame.

There was this moment in late 2018 when Darren and I were going into a huge meeting. We were pumped up, confident, and we'd huddled like a couple of athletes beforehand. Fist bump, quick nod, "We've got this."

We're standing just outside the doorway of where we had just held an amazing meeting and we were about to engage in conversation with some serious players exiting the meeting room, and out of nowhere, I grabbed a hold of Darren's hand ever so gently. Like a weirdo. I guess I thought he was Lee-Ann for a short moment. I don't know what came over me. He reflexively whipped his hand.

"What the hell, man?" He whispered. I think I responded with something like "oh, sorry," and kept my game face on.

Three years later that embarrassing moment constantly pops back up when Darren wants to razz me in front of people, but for the life of me, when I analyze what took place, I can't help but think, "What made me grab his hand?" He's annoyingly handsome, sure, but he sure ain't my type! He's all yours, Stephanie!

I reflect on the Robin Hood thing and the remarks of Henok Msghina and Shelden Smollan: "We're here to completely turn a corrupt, bloated, cutthroat industry upside down," Msghina says. We are the Experior Mafia. We've liberated agents to serve their clients with every conceivable product under the sun that's worth brokering.

Aurelio Evans loves to tell people that his job is a teacher. He says, "I teach How to Build Wealth 101 for a living; it's the class we all missed in school. My job is to give the world this continuing education so that every person I speak with is more educated and informed when I leave. I don't sell products. I teach. The clients become so educated that they choose the products that are right for them. Rather than sell, I empower clients to take personal responsibility for their financial futures."

We're giving people their lives and freedom back. We're helping people dream. We're getting people on their feet. We're making millionaires. We're facilitating retirement. We're giving grandparents and parents the ability to be present with their children. We're keeping roofs over single moms' heads. Damn, no wonder I feel so emotional. The feeling that overcame me when I grabbed Darren's hand in one of the most embarrassing moments I've had at a big event was appreciation, trust, and love that had nothing to do with canoodling. Like Darren pointed out so many months before, it's The Trust Factor. We're just that unified.

Chapter Seventeen

Create a Great Company with Empowered Teammates

"I never won anything by myself. I was always strong because of
help that gave me extra strength to win."
Dan Gable

"Oh, I got into it with Jamie..." Andrea Rogers recalls. The Experior leaders were meeting to discuss the compensation structure you learned about in Chapter Five. What I left out then was the Legacy program that agents like Tzachi Chen and Andrea Rogers fought so hard for.

To preface the story, I'll start with the moral. Lee-Ann and I listen to our agents. We take into account their goals for the company. We run the numbers to give them what they want and need. In some cases, this has to do with commission. Of course, everybody wants more commissions, but our job is to make it at once accessible and also profitable for everybody on the team so that we can continue to expand and develop the internal operations and systems. Our job is to continue to create millionaires for decades to come, as clients and agents, and shareholders, who also happen to be every Executive Director working with us. It's not as easy to "wave a magic wand" as you'd hope when running our complex Tribrid Model of Builders, Career support, and Personal Production opportunity.

From Left to Right: Darren Golka, Andrea Rogers, and Stephanie Golka

When Rogers joined Experior, the legacy program lasted for ten years. Ten years after you left your business, transitioned to a new industry, or passed, your family would still receive income from your business for a decade. That's pretty sweet, right!? 99% of companies in our industry have nothing even comparable to this.

Rogers left her previous company after 18 years with nothing to show for it, but at Experior she faced her final career; she'll be with us until she retires, which will be soon. In-kind, Rogers has built an impressively large organization with Experior, currently at over 150 licensed agents.

"Jamie, our mission statement is, 'Building Financial Foundations for Families Today and Leave a Legacy for Tomorrow,' so if I die today, my grandbaby will be only 12 years old when my legacy runs dry. Legacy is a lifetime."

"Is this even possible?" I later asked Lee-Ann, our accountant, our lawyer, Shelden, our CXO, and a whole suite of experts in the field. "Can this be done?"

Now there's the lesson. I didn't say, "Wow, Rogers. That sounds like a real headache for us. I love being generous, but I'm exhausted from crunching numbers. Can't you just be happy with ten years on your Legacy? I mean, this is better than anyone else in town."

The great leader doesn't say *"but can I...?"* He or she says, *"how will I...?"* Because remember, where there's a will, there's a way.

I wrestled for months. How will we do this? How will we make this contractual and most assuredly payout these agents' families for a lifetime? And what about when the beneficiary of this business proceeds dies, then what... and on and on?

There were some words and there were some intense conversations between strong, courageous Andrea, myself, Lee-Ann, and our ELC (Experior Leadership Council), which at the time consisted of our top seven field leaders in the company. In the end, we made the Legacy program even better. When you transition out of Experior for any reason whatsoever, death, disability, retirement, your family can receive 75% of the income generated in the business you built, *indefinitely*. This is not just for the renewals on insurance contracts, no. This is for the overrides and commissions generated from the organization you have built... Indefinitely! Of course, there are certain thresholds that must be met to build this business, but now everyone has the opportunity to build a dynasty that will last forever. For agents like Rogers, Chen, De Lio, and others who are building a team under the Builder's Model of the Tribrid as opposed to focusing on personal production solely, this model will pay their families a tremendous income for decades to come.

Andrea Rogers at a Women's Event with Experior

There was a moment when I felt uncomfortable about how heated the arguments could get as we tweaked and improved our systems together, but this is what makes us a better company. Everyone has a voice to be heard, and if it makes things better, we are damn sure gonna do it. Today the ELC provides one of the most valuable lessons in building a great company. Andrea Rogers feels even more excited to create what will pay for itself 100 times over, no matter how many generations of Roger's heirs we support. She's even talked about her youngest daughter considering joining her business. But had Lee-Ann and I put our foot down and said, "No, way. That's impossible. Nobody else does that," we wouldn't have the passionate Builder that we have in Rogers.

It's critical to crunch numbers. It's sometimes more critical to evaluate the worth of a passionate, empowered team member.

Well, that fateful day in 2020 when we solidified the enhanced Legacy Program, which opened up a can of worms just six months prior in those debates with Andrea and the ELC, has shown once again that we built this company for the true kings and queens of Experior - our agents. Today, it's become a hallmark of our business and is directly correlated with the success of our business. Thank you, Andrea, for pressing this issue to point to a life-changing decision for everyone.

The Experior Mafia

"Jamie cares about one thing in business: his agents."
Mauro Arturi, Executive Director at Experior Financial Group

Experior agents are vested from Day One in the business and there are multiple tiers of shareholders with the company. What's the selfish reason we do this? It's so that *all* of our amazing Executive Directors will go to bat to make this the absolute best company it can be. Golka regularly visualizes the day we become a billion-dollar, or perhaps a publicly-traded company, and because he's a shareholder, he's not hiding valuable intel from the CEO.

I'm floored at the stories I hear of people slacking off for 60% of their workdays, scrolling social media, or generally wasting time at the water cooler. If your team isn't vested in the success of your business, if there's nothing in it for them but watching a CEO or C-Suite take all the glory, *what else do you expect?*

Part of creating a great team is having a great co-pilot. People will one day write books about Frank, Mauro, Laval, Darren,

Shelden, and hopefully every agent in this book, the same way they write about Apple co-founder Steve Wocznniak or the PayPal Mafia, including Max Levchin, Peter Thiel, Elon Musk, Steve Chen, Reid Hoffman, Chad Hurley, Premal Shah, and others.

Experior has developed a similar "mafia," which isn't a bad joke aimed at Mauro Arturi and Frank De Lio. We have a level of badassery on our team meaning that there's no question people will study our models, our partners, and our startup phase in dozens of books following this first one.

Like Steve Jobs had, Lee-Ann and I have an uncanny ability to bring in the right people around us at the perfect time. When agents learn about who Shelden Smollan is in our industry, they're almost starstruck. I like to say that he was around writing policies for the dinosaurs, and he used to play baseball with Jesus. In short, we call him Moses.

Shelden, unlike the other cats in this book, is not an agent with Experior. He is a board member and the Chief Experience Officer of the company. Oh, and he gets shares in the company too, like all of our teammates can earn. I like to say, "He does everything I hate doing." And he does it very well. He started in the insurance industry in 1974 and has played just about every role there is from selling, running an MGA, working with insurance companies, and developing products with insurance firms. He came to work with us in January 2017, when we were only three years in business. His wife Julie must have thought he was nuts teaming up with this rag-tag army of folks trying to disrupt the industry he has spent his entire adult life working in. We were ecstatic when he accepted our offer. It was like we instantly got the necessary intel to continue along the road of domination and disruption ("Muah ha ha..." in a deep, creepy voice).

Shelden Smollan

Smollan, like Mauro, lives, eats, sleeps, and breathes personal relationships. I'm told that once a week, since they live only five minutes from each other, the two enjoy a glass of scotch together at Shelden's home where undoubtedly, they're collaborating and concocting a plan that will elevate our company and our agents beyond any levels Lee-Ann and I could do on our own.

Should I pay these guys for their happy hour? They wouldn't accept it, and they don't need it. Lee-Ann and I have empowered a team that loves each other, loves Experior, and delights in the collective success of the entire operation. Nobody sheds a tear about my car fetish or when they see Lee-Ann and me moving upwards on the success ladder because we only succeed when others succeed. As President and CEO, Lee-Ann and I earn income in direct proportion to our team. Not a fat salary, or stock options: we are commissioned agents of our business. The way we see it is that if it's good enough for you, it better be good enough for us. And it is! We call this truly equal opportunity for everyone, including us.

A sure sign of trust and love in my organization is when people bring in their families. I mentioned Rogers planting the seed with her youngest daughter; Sophie and Tariq; Stephanie and Darren; Tyrone and Melissa Hinds.

One late evening in March of last year, Mark Ferland got a call from his son. "Dad, just from what I've been hearing and listening to you working, I want to join you in business."

"What intrigues you, son?"

"I love the rags-to-riches story of Jamie and Lee-Ann. I love that they struggled and made things happen. I love that anybody can make it to the top."

Mark and Andrea Ferland, "80's Night" with Experior

Ferland's son studied, sat for, and passed his exam in record time, just two weeks, to become licensed (which is fast in Canada). When seasoned guys like Mark Ferland, who's been in the industry for decades hear from their children that they want to join Experior, I know we've scratched something deeper than recruiting "employees." I don't even like to say that word because we never call our kings and queens employees. We call them business owners, partners, and Executive Directors because that's what they are. And we wouldn't be who we are without them.

Shortly after his son's licensing engagement, I called Mark up to congratulate him.

"Mark, coincidentally, after all of your decades in the industry, why did you join us?" Mark is one of our top producing investment representatives, a tremendous asset to our business.

"I'd heard rumors of your hearts, of your authenticity, and about the faith your agents had in the leadership of you and Lee-Ann." Full circle. We listen to our agents. We adjust the company to make our team happy - and our team succeeds.

Great companies empower their teams. Those teams empower the company. There's a never-ending circle of abundance when you listen to and look out for your team.

Reputation

"Venture capitalists will tell you that they'd rather buy a great team than a great idea."
Joe Kraus. Cofounder, Excite

When Executive Director Adeola Abiodun was looking for a new MGA/IMO, somebody mentioned Experior. At the time, Adeola was looking to leave a company with whom he'd been for nine years. The name Experior was known for excellence, and he'd heard that the advisors were well-trained. Even more importantly, he loved the combination of Building and Producing that he'd heard about with Experior.

One day, he showed up unannounced to our Vaughan, Ontario office where he approached the receptionist and asked, "Can somebody here tell me more about this company?" The receptionist asked Frank De Lio to sit down with Abiodun, who warmly and enthusiastically described his Experior experience. "Well, Mr. De Lio. You caught a big fish today!" Adeola said enthusiastically when he left.

Adeola did his research before making the jump from a company he'd been with for a long time as he was already earning $200,000 there. He says, "I knew I'd be successful, but not 'on the verge of crossing $400,000 of income in just three years' successful!"

Adeola Abiodun at the Experior 2020 Convention

A great company is preceded by a great reputation. You treat your employees well, and they treat their clients well. We feel proud to have built a brand name and image that empowers our agents and makes them feel proud to be with us. Sure, you'll always have competitors try to discredit you, and there's the betrayal that you could experience when you decide to move in your career from former associates. Some agents come to us feeling as though they've been robbed, agents such as Matthew Stewart and Andrea Rogers.

But for every hater, there are a thousand stories of admirers. The haters don't bring us down because there is measurably more excellence than ignorance by our haters out there. There are too many happy families being served by well-educated agents for us to lose credibility by the haters.

Dror David, after being the target of several online hate pages, experienced some poetic justice a few days ago. He was taking his dad to the airport, and he saw a guy wearing a green jacket. At first, he thought it was a cab driver, but saw the crest of a company for whom many of our Executive Directors used to work... and struggle.

Dror, feigning ignorance, approached the man. "Excuse me, can I ask you, are you from XYZ Company?"

"Yes."

"Oh... well... you know I'm in the industry as well. I know that a green jacket commemorates good income and a big hierarchy. Congratulations on all your accomplishments."

"Why, thank you! Where are you from?"

"Experior."

The man suddenly paused, looking almost stunned. "Well, ahem, nice to meet you."

"Have a wonderful day." The man walked away. Experior is a direct threat to that man and his business.

Would he have been wise to say, "You know, young man? I've heard about you guys, and it's been nothing short of colorful. Why don't you and I have a conversation, tell me more about what you're up to over there."

Like Mauro, Frank, and Laval, this man could have the opportunity to quadruple his income doing the same amount of work, and with people he may even enjoy being around - an empowered team of people who genuinely care about one another.

But he didn't. He'd likely bought into the lie that no other company can possibly be better than his. It wasn't up for discussion.

Dror felt some level of vindication in that moment. For all the hateful discussion groups that have been created to slander Dror for having the audacity to build a better life for himself and his family and serve the clients he loves to serve, Dror didn't have to say a word except, "Have a wonderful day." At that moment, he was the bigger man. The team player who showed grace and sportsmanship. I feel proud to raise leaders who act with dignity, even when faced with vicious, scarcity-minded bullies.

I also love a story Executive Director Kevin Purnell, who was in the insurance industry for 30 years before linking arms with us, recently shared with me. He was invited to a very prestigious golf course where PGA tournaments had been run. Back at the clubhouse after a round of golf, he was seated at a banquet table with other financial advisors. Everybody summarily went around the table introducing themselves. "I'm from Royal Bank, I'm from Edward Jones, I'm with the Bank of Montreal...," all large institutions in Canada.

One guy who seemed to have it out for Kevin decided to ask about his "financial background."

"I've got a degree in finance and asset management."

"I'm a former stock trader."

"I attended Oxford studying economic theory."

"And what about you?" Somebody directs the conversation towards Kevin.

"Well, I was a server in a hotel."

"And how does that qualify you for the industry?" Purnell was flabbergasted that somebody would call him out in front of his peers.

"John, can you repeat your qualifications for me?" Purnell wisely asked.

"I have a degree in finance and asset management. I went to university."

"I see," Kevin said. "So, you were nothing more than a student before you got into this. You and I have completed the same courses and have the same precise qualifications. We both started from square one, having come from different paths."

The table cheered. Later Kevin heard, "way to stick it to him!" from his peers.

When Kevin got started in our industry, he studied and took his exams while raising young children with his wife, Pam. Before Experior, as you've seen through over a dozen stories in this book, that wasn't an easy life. Sometimes, it wasn't an easy decade.

Kevin and Pam Purnell

When Kevin shared this story with me, he said, "Jamie, one thing I heard years ago from Art Williams that has served me my whole career is this, 'there's never been a test that will measure the heart and will of a champion.'" I couldn't be prouder of Kevin and Pam and their heart-centered, badass team of empowered kings and queens.

Nourish Entrepreneurship

When Mario Francella was nine years old, he asked his dad for $20. His dad pulled out $100 and said, "Here, head to the store and buy everything the kids at the playing field will love, freezies, candy, sodas, whatever." Back then, the items cost ten or twenty cents, so the $100 went far.

Back at home, Mr. Francella threw everything into a cooler with ice, loaded it into the back of his truck, and drove Mario and the cooler to the park where he left him for the remainder of the day with a sign that read: "Cool Treats - One Dollar."

Mario was elated. "Dad, I made three hundred dollars!" he exclaimed as he bolted towards his dad's truck when Mr. Francella returned.

With a serious face, Mr. Francella took $280 back from his son, gave him the $20 he originally asked for and left Mario with one of the most important lessons of his life. Mario learned that you get what you ask for. As an entrepreneur, Dad kept all the profits. As an employee, Mario kept $20. However, an intrapreneur might say, "Hey boss. I have this crazy idea. If I execute this idea with my skills and creativity, let's split the profits 65/35." Mario would have walked away with $100 to do the same amount of work, not $20. The employee has no control of their income based on performance. The intrapreneur designs a position that rewards them a larger chunk of the pie than the employee, but the entrepreneur keeps the whole pie, doling out money to people as he or she sees fit.

"I own my own business in the financial services industry," Frank De Lio says when people ask him what he does. Does it matter that he's an independent commissioned broker? A financial advisor? That he sells insurance? That he helps people make and save money? That he shows people how to protect their money and retire richly?

According to my agents, absolutely not. They're business owners and that's what attracts people to them. They're not "NY Life," or "John Hancock," or "Chase Bank," or "Bank of England." They're entrepreneurs. They're business owners - emphasis on the owners.

Some of you reading this book are captive insurance agents. Others are financial advisors. Some of you are yoga teachers, doctors, or physical therapists. But in everything you do, you have the opportunity to be one of three things: an entrepreneur, an intrapreneur, or an employee.

Employee, Intrapreneur, Entrepreneur

Employee	Intrapreneur	Entrepreneur
Secure, Steady Paycheck	Secure. Steady Paycheck	Responsible to Earn His/Her Own Paychecks
Limited Decision-Making	Moderate Decision-Making	Full Decision-Making
No risk, Limited Rewards	Moderate Risk, Moderate Rewards	High-Risk, High Reward
No Freedom to Plan Your Day	Freedom to Plan Your Day	Only Accountable to Yourself
No Ownership	Limited Ownership	Full Ownership

There's nothing inherently wrong with being an **Employee**. You're paid to show up. You clock in when you're told, you do what you're told with whom you're told to do it, and you clock out when you're told. There's little risk. You have somebody else who tells you what to do.

The next level is the **intrapreneur.** You work within an organization as an employee or sometimes, an independent contractor, but you're motivated to win for the team. You create your own schedule and have a stake in the projects you take on. Because you are your own boss within an organization, there's more risk if you screw up; there's less to blame on a boss. In addition, you miss out on bonuses or commissions you've worked for as an intrapreneur, so there's more accountability.

Finally, the **Entrepreneur**. Entrepreneurship is experiencing a bit of a heyday now with industries such as technology and information marketing, where anybody can sell anything with virtually no credentials. The reward is high, but so is the risk. Entrepreneurs don't have a boss, but the smart ones have close relationships with industry leaders or business coaches. They aren't accountable to anybody throughout their day, so it's critical that they stay self-motivated. Entrepreneurship has a high rate of failure, but the successes are astronomical compared to being an employee or intrapreneur.

At Experior, we've chosen to create a culture of entrepreneurs. Although we have more than 30 Head Office employees and 15+ subcontracted staff for technology, they all think of themselves Intrepreneurs; they're incentivized to take personal responsibility for their days. While Lee-Ann is a fantastic manager, and I am not, she easily manages those employees from home (due to so many lock-downs in Canada from the Covid19 Pandemic), and because of their self-motivated nature, she didn't struggle with the transition in 2020 from Head Office to home, although she misses buying lunch for everybody daily and the communion they shared during that time.

Our company thrives because we attract entrepreneurs like Tzachi Chen, who's building his business with the McDonald's Real Estate Model in mind, or Mario Francella, who banged on up to 100 doors daily when he started his catering business. Or even Dr. Meri and Erik, who host some of the most creative marketing and recruiting events I've ever seen. Experior is for entrepreneurs.

Empowered Teammates are Emotionally Mature

More than once, I've mentioned that Experior is really a personal development company with a great compensation package. That's why I seek to cultivate emotionally mature agents in our numerous weekly team training sessions.

A healthy indication of emotional maturity is the ability to compete. No crybabies. Nobody is running to Lee-Ann complaining that I was mean to them. No victims. We're players, fighters, and winners.

A consummate example of healthy competition is Team REOS (Realizing Each Other's Success) and Team FML (Free My Life). Darren & Stephanie Golka set their sights on passing up Frank De Lio and then Mauro Arturi from Team FML. They really razz each other. At a few points, I worried they were really at odds with each other for about a year, but in the end, there was a lot of love and respect. Golka is passionate about living and working in an environment where leaders can work together, not oppose each other. Considering Golka's C-Level success in his previous business and his massive organization within Experior, I'd say he's one to watch.

One day, when I worried he was getting under Team FML's skin, I asked him if he felt comfortable with FML fighting back, bragging about beating him in numbers. "Iron sharpens iron, brother. Recognize Each Other's Successes. I'm proud of them."

Chapter Eighteen

Create A Great Company with Purpose

"It is not enough to be happy to have an excellent life.
The point is to be happy while doing things that stretch our skills,
that help us grow and fulfill our potential."
Mihaly Csikzentmihalyi

Once you have a why, you'll figure out the how.

Probably due to a lack of anything else meaningful to say in small talk, we ask one another commonly, "so, what do you do?" Next time you get that question, I challenge you to respond like this: "I can tell you *what* I do, but what really excites me is *why* I do it."

I'm the CEO at Experior Financial Group, but why I do it is more compelling. There's no entrance exam to calling yourself a CEO; every other person on LinkedIn has it in their profiles, but less than a fraction of them actually meet the qualifications of a CEO. Newsflash: just because you have a website that you put together in your mom's basement, that doesn't make you a CEO.

For me, the title isn't as important as why I do it. I'm on a mission to show people to keep dreaming the way I dreamt of being on that Cheerios box or making it to the Olympics in wrestling. My Why is to help those dreamers return to their original paths and connect with their birthrights of prosperity, which doesn't generally mean working a soul-sucking job, nine-to-five.

I often illustrate to my team that a human being can live for 40 days without food, four days without water, four minutes without oxygen, but only four seconds without hope. Don't try this at home!

Ask me that question again. "Mr. Prickett, what do you do for a living?"

"I'm a hope dealer." My hope to change an entire industry and over a million lives helps me commit the consistency and sacrifice needed to grow my company.

It's more compelling than happy hour. It's sexier than the four-hour working week. It's more valuable than a million-dollar annual bonus for clocking in and out of a company that I don't believe in.

As I type this, there's a study that just came out in Canada that indicates we have over one million vacant jobs as people exit the workforce. It's also the case in the United States, I've read. It's being called The Great Resignation.

One of my lifelong best friends since Grade Three, Daryl Toonk, just got walked out of his place of employment after 15 years because he won't comply with rules he cannot follow for personal reasons. He was literally walked off the job a few weeks ago as I type this.

People have the luxury of realizing that there's more to life than a job. There's nothing more beautiful than to see people hitting the reset button on life, even if they walk out under trying circumstances. It's beautiful to live in a world where there's hope. Where you can get five days a week back in your life because you chose to.

What was Daryl looking for? What are you looking for? You're looking for that same thing that won't let Shelden Smollan retire in peace - not now. That same thing that Mark Ferland and Neela Mannan are bringing their kids along for; the same thing Tariq and Editha have enlisted for, along with their spouses. You're looking for something that you can sink your teeth into that's challenging, but still possible. A game worth winning - not a race on a hamster wheel. You want Flow in your life.

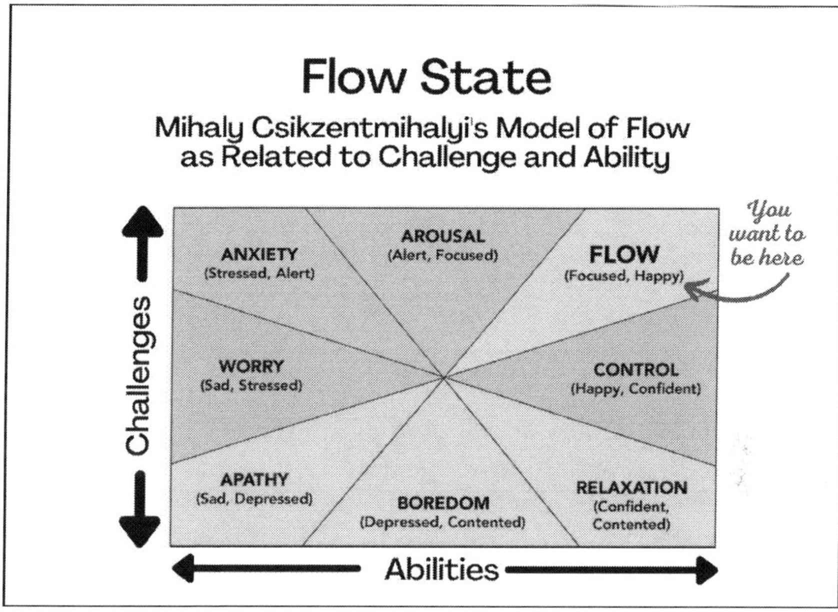

We Share in One Another's Why's

"When the why is big enough, the how will figure itself out."
Darren Golka, Executive Director at Experior

Executive Director Madhab Dulal was born and raised in Nepal and had an otherwise average high school and university experience. He came to Canada and worked in a Walmart warehouse as a Quality Assurance Associate, where you may remember he walked away when he learned that his income ceiling peaked at just $70,000 annually.

Dulal is one of the first faces I see in my head when somebody says the word purpose. In Nepal, there's a heartbreaking practice of kicking parents out of the home when a child is married or otherwise independent. Millions of these men and women suffer lives on the streets. There's no better example of a region that is in desperate need of senior care, which is already a dire global need.

Dulal himself didn't take any property from his parents; he chose to forego his inheritance to give his parents freedom. But he wanted to do more for the parents in Nepal, of whom he claims 80-90% percent are suffering.

Dulal founded the Hope House, where he's adopted several Nepalese moms and dads. Even though he only joined Experior two years ago, he was promoted to Executive Director and has already surpassed the $250,000 annual income mark. Nothing stopped Dulal, including the pandemic which arrived soon after he joined.

Shortly after Dulal joined, I asked him, "What is it that drives you this hard? What's motivating you?"

"I am passionate about financial education. All I do is learn about markets. I may never be an English teacher, but I can tell anybody how money works, with expertise."

"There's more..." I pressed. That's when he told me that he won't stop until he has the $10 million he needs to make a real dent in the Nepalese senior care crisis. Hope House is his "why".

"Nobody else is going to do it for me, for those parents being kicked out on the street," he said, matter of factly.

I didn't grab his hand, but I definitely wanted to give him a hug. "That's exactly what it is, thank you for allowing me to be on *your* team, Madhab."

When your team has their own why's and purposes beyond anything I could fabricate or drill into them, that's when you've superseded manipulation and you've entered the realm of motivation. Madhab is wholeheartedly, unstoppably, obsessively motivated to change the world. Just like Tariq and Sophie, and Daniel Prete, who won't let another couple like his parents nearly lose everything on account of some slimy financial advisor while on his watch. Or Frank De Lio, who saw the horror in his own mother's eyes when she learned that an agent had sold her and Mr. De Lio a bill of goods.

There are two main ways our agents build their organizations within Experior. They focus on either recruiting (the Builder Model) or service (Personal Producer Model), or a combination of both, as they go hand in hand. Mark Ferland dominates with the Personal Producer Model and Tzachi Chen is soaring with the Builder Model.

Even though I'm focused on agents and Mauro is focused on his organization as opposed to individual clients and transactions, we're both ultimately here to change the lives of the end-user: our clients. When our agents succeed, the clients succeed. This liberates me to stay single-focused in my personal flow-state of running the business. There's a chef, a dishwasher, a front-of-house manager, servers, and a bartender (which is apparently Shelden Smollan), and we're all cooking up a feast to deliver to the diners at the tables. As the chef, I don't always see or interact with the diners - but I put my entire soul into their meals.

When I started in the sales industry, I didn't understand what I was selling. I was 21 years old and bought my first life insurance policy one Sunday afternoon in late June 2001.

The agent asked me the magic question, "do you know anyone interested in earning extra income or starting their own business?"

"Pick me!" I thought. I was working in a factory at a soul-sucking job. He didn't need to promise me millions of dollars, a private island with a 300-foot yacht. He just needed to give me a glimmer of hope that I could escape that factory. That I wouldn't be like my best friend Daryl, who spent 15 years in a job only to be forced to walk away one day, willing to give it all up in an instant.

The agent then told me about a Tuesday evening meeting I could attend about an hour away from my home. I walked into an office that Tuesday night and saw a hundred or so other people sitting in a meeting room, staring at a projection screen with the company name on it. The presentation was, of course, compelling. I knew this was my shot.

Although I had some reservations, I began attending training classes and seminars, becoming a licensed life insurance agent. I listened to everything the company told me. However, I didn't do any outside research or homework. I spent 45 days listening to training tapes and absorbing what other successful people in the company shared. I honestly believed that I was on a crusade to spread the truth about the life insurance industry and that this company was *the only one* that everybody should do business with.

I wasn't even aware that there were hundreds of other companies and thousands of other products out there to meet client needs. I was brainwashed into believing that agents with other companies were unethical within a year. Within two years, I believed it should be illegal to solicit what other companies sold. I theorized that the government was in bed with the insurance industry because the wealthy insurance industry paid all the taxes. Here I was, on a crusade to correct the injustice.

However, I didn't do a lot of research outside of the bubble I had put myself into. I believed what people spoon-fed to me from people who drilled it into them, going back to what had been drilled into them from the top down.

Multiplied propaganda can make even the wisest person believe a lie. When I left a ten-year career with that company, countless people were shocked. I'd invested ten years telling everyone how great that company was, how no other company could do it better, and how other companies were downright evil. Yes, I actually said that.

You see when this happened, people were hurt. Had I been lying? No, I had been deceived. But because of that deception, I perpetuated a myth. I perpetuated propaganda. People were threatened. Lee-Ann and I were setting out to build a new agency that would be a direct competitor with my former peers.

People were disgusted. I had said that anybody who sold for another company was evil.

People felt betrayed. Friends felt like if I wasn't with them, that I was against them.

I want to share with you how this has even been relevant in sports.

Lebron James couldn't win a championship with the Cleveland Cavaliers, so he left them in 2010 and went on to win two Championships with the Miami Heat. Did his fans in Cleveland shout praises of glory when this occurred? No! He went from hero to hated over the course of a summer during the trade. Fast forward four years, he goes back to Cleveland. For the fans of Cleveland now, he goes from hated to hero, and then takes Cleveland to the finals four times, and wins one Championship with them during his second coming. He's a Hero, and then he decides to go to the Los Angeles Lakers, and guess what? See below:

Let's look at Lebron James through the eyes of a typical Cleveland Cavalier Fan

Lebron James Career history

2003–2010	HERO	Cleveland Cavaliers
2010–2014	HATED	Miami Heat
2014–2018	HERO AGAIN	Cleveland Cavaliers
2018-Present	HATED AGAIN	Los Angeles Lakers

Now, although I am not personally a fan of Lebron James (after all, we all know Michael Jordan is the GOAT), I can see that he was on a mission to win championships. You see that the crusade of winning a championship and Lebron being the hero is alive and well when the team has him on their side, but when he leaves, the confusion sets in. Why did he leave? Was it money? Was it a lack of loyalty? Was it because he never really cared about us? Was he just about the talk? You see, confusion sets in, and even hate can set in in some cases over the silliest of things that have no impact over our lives. One of the biggest causes of this is that multiplied propaganda can make even the wisest person believe a lie.

At some point, you're going to make a decision to follow your own inner compass, and some people will berate and bully you like my former company and so many former companies have done to my agents. But to rise above that abuse, it's critical that we stay laser-focused on our purpose.

Mauro Arturi lost his best friend of 37 years when he left his former company. It breaks his heart. But he's on a mission. When you're driven by authentic purpose; when you're motivated (not manipulated) by great leaders with an honest cause, nothing can hold you back. It may feel like a war in the trenches sometimes, but you wouldn't have it any other way.

Chapter Nineteen

Let Your Haters Be Fuel

"The only way to get people to stop talking about you and making you feel like crap is to do nothing."
Jamie Prickett

"When a person or group of unsuccessful people can't stop hating on someone who's wealthier, more successful, and better than they are in every way imaginable they are said to have been drinking (hateraide)- as to how long the hating lasts depends on how much hateraide they consume, which can be a lot. 'The group of losers decided to hate on the most successful person. Must have been drinking that hateraide.'"
Urban Dictionary

Trash talking has always motivated me. It must be the sweaty, bruised-up years I spent on the wrestling mat. It fuels me and it's one of the greatest blessings I can give to my team: to develop a mental callous.

For kicks, here are just a few of the barbs I've encountered just in the past few months.

"Experior is in hot water; they're going to go under."

"The Pricketts get rich by stealing from their agents."

"They don't pay their agents enough; they'll never last." and conversely, "They pay their agents too much, they'll never last."

Excuse me while I choke on my eleventh cup of coffee today. I went back and forth with my editor for a month on whether or not I should even mention the financial success of our agents; the Madhab Dulals who earned $250,000 annually in just two years. The multiple men and women who never exceeded six figures in previous insurance agencies but who are now earning $100,000, $250,000, and $500,000 milestones - all of whom have been with us for between just one to six years. Oh yeah, I forgot to mention, the first two years we only had one six-figure earner, and she quit during the lawsuit with the Practice Company!

They didn't come with a trust fund. They came here with hope. Moving on...

"They only recruit the low-hanging fruit." That would be accurate. I grab the fruit that's ripe; the fruit you want to eat. I grab the stuff that's ready.

"Oh, you mean Bhupinder's business?" Implying that Lee-Ann and I didn't build this business, but rather a gentleman named Bhupinder did. Although, that would also be accurate. We're nothing without Bhupinder and our remarkable team, but Bhupinder joined us four years after we were already rocking and rolling.

My agents commonly come to me bruised and beaten down by insecure haters who flog them for leaving their companies, especially from the insurance and network marketing spaces. I find myself regularly sharing this speech:

"You know, as athletes, we have calluses on our hands, feet, elbows. We have hard skin on our bodies. If I jumped into the gym and started lifting heavy on my first day, what would happen? They might bring me out in a stretcher at my age, and I'd surely have rips on my hands from the soft skin getting shredded by the iron bars. This is your moment to develop a hard skin on your mind; a mental callous."

My wrestling comeback after partying for years in my 20's

It's beyond "don't sweat the small stuff." When your team understands how to gracefully ignore haters, the haters become fuel. You don't ignore it. You take every nugget of hatred and devour it; it energizes and nourishes you.

I remind my agents that for every hater, there are a thousand people who need them to stay focused on their Whys.

One of the many things I love about haters is the publicity. That public slander is just about the best marketing in the world. And it's free! The right people won't take things at face value, but they'll get curious. Those critical thinkers are the people you want to attract.

When I left my previous company, a woman I'd known for years sent me a Facebook message that I've hesitated about including in this book, even now on the eve before my final manuscript is due. But here it is. She wrote,

> *"I am shocked. I trusted you. I believed you. I thought you wanted to be a good person. You are a hypocrite, a liar, selfish and self-centered. You don't care about anyone but yourself. You need help. And you are NOT a Christian. Thank you though.... you leaving is the best thing that ever happen (sic) to me. I have learned more and gotten more out of the two months in John's baseshop (agency) than I did in 2 years with you. You are a disgrace."*

I've commenced big lectures by posting that vicious message on the screen. People in the audience, accustomed to an enthusiastic, silly, light-hearted, and encouraging leader invariably looked perplexed.

I think it's important that my team and you all understand that following your heart and gut doesn't always engender everyone to you. When I received that message on Facebook, I cried. I didn't shake it off overnight, and it took even longer to forgive this former friend. But if I hadn't forgiven this lady and moved on, I assure you Experior wouldn't be here today.

Developing a mental callous doesn't mean denying your pain or pretending the nasty words weren't spoken. It means moving that pain through your spirit and body so that you can continue with your dream.

Lee-Ann and I had a dream to create the greatest financial services company in the country, and now the world. We spent a combined 16 years working with a company that bamboozled us. Worst of all, thousands of men and women around were struggling to pay their bills. In a perfect world, we could have taken them all with us. But if you know anything about mass formation or totalitarian dictatorships, a good 30% of those convinced souls were so certain of their rightness that they wouldn't come if we'd paid them a million dollars.

God doesn't make junk. Even your haters are divine masterpieces. You can respect them and handle their hatred with grace. You can let the pain be your teacher. You can transmute the trauma into wisdom. But that doesn't mean you have to codependently let that hatred control you. Move the energy into love and let it go.

I'll go back to the concept of being positively brainwashed. A man who used to share an office with me once said, "Jamie will be washing dishes for a living by the end of the year."

On a conference call with the CEO from our competitor company, where there were over 100,000 agents around the time I'd brought Frank, Mauro, and Laval on board. He said, "these knuckleheads haven't been in business for six months, and they're not gonna last six months."

I got a suit jacket embroidered with "knuckleheads" on the inner collar, and today I keep a photo of my wife and me back in the day with that gentleman on my desk where I scribbled "knuckleheads" across the photo.

Another whale tried to recruit me to his large company when Experior was just two years old. I replied, "sorry, I can't work for a company that compensates the agents the way yours does."

He said, "Jamie, I'm fixin' for you to be the captain of the ship. Now some people like to be out there in the big deep ocean with their rickety little tugboat because they own them. But I'm offering you to be the captain of the ship."

Today, I have a picture of a tugboat on my wall. Tugboats are the saviors of the big ships in the ocean. Tugboats motivate me.

Why Not?

"I guess the guy who won just wanted it more than you."
Larry Prickett (my Dad)

"Fear is like fire. You can use it to drive you. It can burn you, but it can also feed you and it can help you."
-UFC Bantamweight Fighter, Jasmine Jasudavicius

To this day, I thank my dad for infusing me with the heart of a champion. I thought he was tough when he let me know that if I wanted to be an Olympic wrestler, I couldn't settle for 2nd place. I never did get the Gold, but today I'm fighting for something which is having a bigger impact on the world than me being an

Olympian. Experior Financial Group will one day become the number one financial services company in the world.

I must also say, I am so thankful to Mom, who has believed in me no matter what. Whether I told her I was going to win the Olympics, become a billionaire, or change the world, she believed in me.

As a wrestler, it was all about me. But with Experior, I'm fighting with and for the thousands of agents we're onboarding, and the millions of families' lives we'll change, and are already changing.

The game hasn't changed, but my Why has. As a new agent at 21 years old, I was in it for "gold and glory." Eventually, after getting mud on my face and struggling just to stay above water in the industry for ten years, my dream had shrunk to "gas and groceries." But I'm the same guy playing the same game: a mental game. I've heard that 90% of winning is a mental game, and I think it may even be proven. It sure has proven true for my life.

At 21 years old, I started in this industry. I had a kid, a mortgage, and was married. But I only made $13,000 that year. It wasn't until eleven years into the industry, and four years after I met Lee-Ann, that I started making enough money to get by, but certainly not enough to counteract the previous decade of struggle. Not until Experior. Not until the Tribrid. Not until the freedom we have to serve our clients and one another, here.

Again, the game didn't change, but my Why did, and then I started winning. I remember one of those infamous moments when I was about seven or so years into the Practice Company and I could barely put gas in my car and I was behind on rent. I was just leaving a client's house and was in tears on the ride home and said to myself, "I can't leave this industry. The world needs me."

As a young boy, Russell Westbrook Jr. and I had one thing in common, and it wasn't a size 14 shoe entering high school. It's not even our shared impeccable sense of fashion. Russell's Mom and Dad famously trained their sons, Russell Jr. and Raynard, to never say, "Why me?" but to instead look at everything in life that you want to achieve and ask yourself, "Why not?" This left such an impact on Russell. He was the underdog when he started playing basketball in high school. Then he was an underdog playing in the NCAA. He even began his NBA career, again, as an underdog. But he kept asking himself, "Why not?" At just 24 years old, Westbrook began the Why Not Foundation; a charity that is committed to helping struggling youth turn their "Why Mes" into "Why Nots."

Today, that little boy, Russell Jr who asked *why not?* is a two-time NBA All-Star Game Most Valuable Player. He's a nine-time NBA All-star and holds the NBA scoring record two times, in the seasons 2014-2015 and again in 2016-2017. Westbrook was subsequently named the NBA's Most Valuable Player in the 2016-2017 season and went on to lead the league in assists in the 2017-2018 season.

Westbrook also became one of only two players in NBA history to average a triple-double in his 2017 season, joining Oscar Robertson, who achieved the feat in 1962. Westbrook also set a record for the most triple-doubles in a season, a record that had stood firmly for 55 years. Then, in 2021 he did the impossible, by-passing Oscar for the most career triple-doubles, a record that many NBA commentators and journalists are on record years ago stating "It is a record that will be impossible for anyone in 'today's' NBA to break."

Russell Westbrook has consistently asked himself "why not?"

It's easy to look at your upbringing or family and say, "Nobody in my family has ever done this, why would I be any different?" *Why me?*

And to that I say: *why not?*

When I first saw Russell Westbrook on TV, I thought, "Look at his clothes! He looks like a clown!" If you're laughing right now, it's because you know that I'm a bit of an eccentric dresser, certainly not one to wear a suit and tie with fancy dress shoes.

The day before our 2019 Experior Annual convention, a pair of Russell Westbrook Air Jordans were released. They were called *Why Not?* You better believe I grabbed a pair of these shoes.

The following day I wore these colorful basketball shoes at the largest conference we'd ever had at the time, along with a tailored white suit. People were a bit confused with my choice of attire until, at the end of the night, I shared what is considered by some to be my most impactful speech. The crazy part was that it wasn't until the morning of the convention that I had decided to scrap everything I had already prepared for weeks in advance and felt compelled to share the Russell Westbrook story. I was sharing the vision that Russell Westbrook has for underprivileged youth, and how he teaches them what his parents taught him - stop asking yourself why, and start asking WHY NOT?

It's impossible to conclude this book for many reasons. There are still 1,700 agents stories to be told in volumes two, three, four, and beyond. Experior is still brand new. Our vision is to build the largest, most powerful team of agents ever to hit the world.

Why Not?

Why will our agents dominate their competitors, devouring them swiftly and finally?

Why not?

The industry, and the world, deserve the integrity Experior brings.

Why should we create financial freedom for families who've been duped by agents held captive to what Daniel Prete called "1970s financial instruments?"

Why not?

Why do we create efficiency and excellence where the market has provided inadequate, insufficient, and limited product offerings to people who need real solutions?

Why not?

Even though building a $50 million company in eight years may sound like a story in and of itself, this is only the introduction. Why will we become a multibillion-dollar company?

Why not?

Over the coming years, you'll hear many more stories of the Experior Mafia. Lee-Ann and I may even collaborate on another book someday, but we'd rather shine the light on the team. We haven't given the men and women of Experior fish so that they may eat for a day. We've taught them how to fish so that they can feast for life.

Why not?

Something you may not know is that it was actually really uncomfortable for me to write this book. I'm not one to take a lot of credit, which is why the stories herein revolve around others. It's really not about me or Lee-Ann. It's about this team. Like Mauro said, "Jamie lives for his agents. Period." You can live to serve others and still be a huge success.

Why not?

Money doesn't motivate me the way that changing lives does. Like that moment I considered giving up after years of struggling. I didn't. I wouldn't. I couldn't. I knew that God put me in this industry to change the world. You can live out your destiny.

Why not?

My Russell Westbrook Why Not? Air Jordan's

I'll spend a weekend on stage motivating agents before a day at the racetrack any day. UFC or Basketball, well, that's another story. *But this is my why, my purpose if you will, and if you have a purpose, you can easily change Why Mes into Why Nots.*

On that note, let's revisit one more epic moment in time that I just shared. January 2019. I'm on stage in a white suit with a crisp silver shirt and my Russell Westbrook Why Not Air Jordan's.

I transitioned in that moment from speaker to preacher. My heart usually pounds on stage with excitement, but on this night, I looked out at the audience and see Lee-Ann sitting with a characteristically calm, confident expression on her face.

Just behind her, I see Frank De Lio, who'd only been with us at that time for three years. He was standing up cheering and waving a white cloth napkin in the air from the table he was at. I'm not sure why, but at that moment when I saw Frank's face and completely broke the script. Anytime you're moved to break the script, good things are to come, eh?

At this moment, I was about 10 minutes into my talk, and I began preaching like Eric Thomas or maybe more like Bishop T.D. Jakes,

"Five years ago this January, Experior was born. Our first Grand Opening had six people who bothered to make the trip to Guelph. We struggled, but we kept going. I had a CEO from a company I came from tell his senior leaders on a conference call that we were a bunch of knuckleheads; don't pay any attention to them. They're not gonna last six months in business."

I continued, "Guys, I was told by another guy, this guy used to rent an office from me at the Practice Company. Ya know what he said to his teammates? He said that Jamie would be doing dishes by the end of the year. Then, one day, Rochelle got a call at our office from a friend of hers that used to work at the Practice Company. Her friend said, 'I hear there's a lawsuit. I hear they're gonna destroy you guys and shut you down. Aren't you worried about your job?' Guess what? We didn't listen to the haters!

"The only way for people not to talk about you? Don't do anything! That's it. Just don't get around to doing nothing, then people will have nothing to talk about. Here we are, approaching a thousand licensed agents. We're just a pee hole in the snow. We're just getting started."

Then I asked the crowd, "But do you know what?"

The audience replied in unison, "WHAT?"

"We broke records in every single area that we do business,

and we have been breaking records every single quarter since the day Experior was born!"

Cheers erupted!

I went on, "Guys, your playing small doesn't serve the world. Maybe you want to ask me Jamie, was it worth it? Every canceled appointment; every person who quit; everyone that said we wouldn't make it; every lie told about us and to us; every bill payment missed; every sacrifice we made; every single bit of the tough stuff that we all went through, that all of us leaders have gone through...I'm telling you: *it's worth it...*

"You want to make a thousand a week, part-time? You want to make ten thousand a week? You want to make ten thousand a day? You want to make ten thousand an hour, Frank? Why Not?

"You want a net worth of $10 million? Why Not? $100 million net worth? Why Not? You want to be a billionaire? Why Not? Someone told you you can't? Someone told you you'd be washing dishes next year? Someone told you you're crazy? Stop letting haters rent space in your head and start evicting them. Stop asking why, and start asking why not?

"You see, most agents didn't come to us as super successful agents. Many had no experience whatsoever. And the ones that came with experience were so beat up and dying for some light in their life!"

The passion and excitement were so amazing at that moment, that even the waiting staff and people working the room at the venue had chills. Many of them mentioned afterward how it made them feel. But I'm going to direct the final closing of this speech towards you now, the reader.

You see many of our leaders simply found their voice. They learned to dream big again They learned to believe that anything is possible. They learned that failure isn't final, but a necessary step to achieve success. And then, they began helping more families. And yes, their bank account certainly reflects it. You might ask "why?" To that I say, "Why not!?"

Dear reader, I want you to start living your Why Not life.

Do you want to retire your parents? *Why Not?*

Do you want to spend more time with your children? *Why Not?*

Do you want a net worth of $10 million? *Why Not?*

Do you want to make $10,000 an hour? *Why Not?*

But do you know what most people want? They want time, and they want to make a difference. And building a successful business can give you both!

Stop saying, "Oh, the men and women in this book started years ago. I'll never catch up."
Stop saying, "My parents were broke, or I came from a broken home."
Stop saying, "I'm not smart enough."
Stop saying, "I'm not pretty enough."
Stop saying, "I'm not confident enough."
Stop saying, "I'm not young enough."
Stop saying, "I'm not old enough."
Stop saying, "I'm not ________________ (Insert whatever excuse you can think of here)!"

Stop being afraid of your own power.

Accept the plan that God has for YOU to change your world and the world for others.

Stop asking yourself, "Why me?" and start asking yourself, "Why Not?"

Epilogue

Thank you for joining Lee-Ann, myself, and just a few of the Experior Financial Group team members in this book that celebrates Great Leadership, Great Companies, and the opportunity we all have to shake up industries that have been operating at low levels of consciousness. Now consider: what would a world look like for your parents, your children, your best friend, or your peers if they were the beneficiaries of companies operating with generosity, heart, flexibility, and integrity?

Help me create that world. Here's how you can share You Can't Fall Off The Floor with people you love.

1. Write an amazing five-star review wherever you purchased this book and/or wherever you love buying books.

2. Ask your local bookstore to stock You Can't Fall Off The Floor. This helps us get more inspiration and positive change into your local community.

3. Run a You Can't Fall Off The Floor Mastermind with peers. Spend several weeks discussing each step in Parts Two and Three of this book.

Great Leaders

1. Great Leaders Use Motivation, Not Manipulation
2. Great Leaders Value Mindset Over Skillset
3. Great Leaders Make Promises They Can Keep
4. Great Leaders Keep Evolving
5. Great Leaders Listen
6. There's No Job Too Small for a Great Leader
7. Great Leaders Inspire Others

Great Companies

1. Create a Great Company with Equal Opportunities for All
2. Create a Great Company as a Family
3. Create a Great Company as a Family
4. Create a Great Company with Continually Evolving Products
5. Create a Great Company with Empowered Teammates
6. Create a Great Company with Purpose
7. Let Your Haters Be Fuel

4. Learn more about Experior and how to plug into our culture, our free online training, and even join our team by heading over to www.experiorfinancial.com or scan this QR Code:

5. To watch a video about our business, head over to www.experiorusavideo.com or www.experiorcanadavideo.com

6. Join us on YouTube. To see more stories of our Executive Directors (and a video of me rapping to Ice Ice Baby on stage), go here:

7. Purchase a copy of You Can't Fall Off The Floor for everybody you love at your favorite online bookstore. Visit www.JamiePrickett.com to score your copy.

Love,
Jamie Prickett

Made in the USA
Monee, IL
14 December 2022

48d530f7-3e19-4f9d-8b5e-1df7d5346d9cR01